ELWOOD GLOVER'S LUNCHEON DATES

Courtesy of CKEY, Toronto

ELWOOD GLOVER'S LUNCHEON ☆ DATES ☆

ELWOOD GLOVER

A James-Christen Book

Prentice-Hall of Canada, Ltd.,
Scarborough, Ontario

© 1975 James-Christen Associates

ALL RIGHTS RESERVED
No part of this book may be reproduced in any form
without permission in writing from the publishers.

Prentice-Hall, Inc., Englewood Cliffs, New Jersey
Prentice-Hall International, Inc., London
Prentice-Hall of Australia, Pty., Ltd., Sydney
Prentice-Hall of India, Pvt., Ltd., New Delhi
Prentice-Hall of Japan, Inc., Tokyo

ISBN 0-13-274498-8

For permission to quote from the following works the publisher
is grateful: page 106, Connors-Walsh wedding service, with permission
of the Reverend Beverley Leslie; page 109, "On Being Canadian" by Keath
Barrie, © 1975 United Artists Music (Canada) Limited; page 109
"Changes" by Terry Rowe, © 1975 Lester and Orpen Limited;
page 43, from "My Heart Soars" by Chief Dan George, © 1975
Hancock House; page 168, "Those Days of Summer" by Leon Bibb, © 1973
Leon Bibb Productions Limited.
"My thanks to the CBC for permission to use
comments from interviews on *Luncheon Date
with Elwood Glover.*"

Design and Production/Maher & Garbutt Ltd.

5 4 3 2 1 AP 75 76 77 78 79

Printed and bound in Canada

TO...

Beth
Hazel
Nancy
Leslie
Sandra
Carol
Janet
Barbara

Herb
Ed
Bill
Stewart
Bob
Nigel
Drew
Terry

Shane
Jack
Alex
Athan

If they'd taken their vows they couldn't have been more dedicated.

Who fought bravely through all the insanity to turn it out every day.

To Len and John whose fault it was in the first place.

To Christine and Patricia who patiently and miraculously read my handwriting.

September 1975

FOREWORD

Anybody can start a book but it takes real guts to finish it, to stand up and be counted for the fool you are.

ARTIE SHAW ON "LUNCHEON DATE" 1961

It seems that for sixty years of my life I managed to resist the temptation to become an author. Temptation?

For fourteen years of my life I interviewed authors – hundreds of them, male and female – on the average of two or three a week. In almost every case the authors seemed to be perfectly ordinary people, just like your next-door neighbor or someone who lives on the next street over. Not one of the hundreds had the overwhelming "I am . . ." aura that often marks the show business star and always cloaks the nobility. They were ordinary people who had a story to tell and chose to tell it in print.

The temptation may have been there subconsciously but there was no way I was going to indulge it. I was a product of the spoken word, not the printed one. However, in the spring of 1975 as my tenure with the "Luncheon Date" television program was coasting to a conclusion, a publisher contacted me with an interesting proposition: Would I be prepared to share with readers my experiences as a host and interviewer?

Why not? Except the spoken word is so comfortably fleeting; the written one is permanent for posterity to record and judge. But again, why not indeed? I'm sure publishers pore over the *Guinness Book of Records* for someone newsworthy – who has not only built a better mousetrap but one with an indoor sauna and automatic cheese dispenser!

So why not a book about a television program and how it got that way? A coffee-table book maybe, with lots of pictures? Gift buying is big business these days: for

Christmas, payoffs for social obligations, to woo clients, to woo girls; what better token of esteem is there in the benevolent world of commerce than the coffee-table book? But, then I thought of Roloff Beny and Emil Schultess who have elevated the coffee-table book to a fine art. How about something for Aunt Milly in a rest home who was a fan of "Luncheon Date" from away back and who with her tray beside her considered the program a necessary part of her diet? That's what we'll do, a handy bit of nostalgia to thumb through during an idle hour, the very thing to prop the door back or to serve as a pad to catch the water stains of a potted plant. Functional – that's what we want. The fact that Bruce Lowry, a devoted fan, took hundreds of pictures during "Luncheon Date's" run was the final inducement.

Sorry, Ted Baxter, it was not a "little 5,000-watt station in Fresno where it all started." It was a 250-watt station in Moose Jaw, Saskatchewan, where a starry-eyed kid approached his first microphone with awe and said silently, "This is for me." Back in those mid-thirties depression days settling on a career was far from easy. And with radio holding such utter fascination for me, it was my life-line during that bleak era which held so little hope for the future.

But I'm ahead of my story.

So, here I am. I have come to terms with my dilemma and if curiosity is part of your make-up I hope this confrontation is worthwhile. During my years in television I often thought "Luncheon Date" played to a largely captive audience; you were either a fan or you avoided it like the plague. When I suggested to the publisher that the front cover of this book should contain an on-off switch, he treated the suggestion as an interesting idea until he thought of the circulation. Anyway, I've yielded. Now I leave you on your own.

ELWOOD GLOVER
September 1975

CONTENTS

Foreword — vii

1 "What am I doing… — 1
An account – among other things – of how I got the bird.

2 Somewhere back there… — 23
A nostalgic journey through the early days of radio.

ACTORS — 41

3 The rumors swirled… — 59
How I thwarted an attempt to poison me in my early TV days.

COMICS — 113

4 I wish I could… — 121
This is a mash note from me to all of "Luncheon Date's" critics.

MOVERS & DOERS — 129

5 The morning of 31 May '73… — 149
The spookiest day of my life and why I decided to abdicate from television.

MUSICIANS — 157

6 I recall reaching… — 175
The decision to leave "Luncheon Date" and how I reached it.

ELWOOD GLOVER'S LUNCHEON DATES

1

★★★★★★★★★★★★★★★★★★★★★★★★★★★

WHAT AM I DOING...

... here? The thought flashed through my mind as I lay sprawled on the studio floor on my back. A "Luncheon Date" cameraman framed my kicking legs and feet – it looked like the frenetic farewell of an ungainly bird. It *was* a bird – an emu, in fact – that had put me into this unusual position.

I was interviewing this emu and he turned ... well, perhaps I should start at the beginning.

One of the more entertaining shows to play the O'Keefe Centre in Toronto during 1974 was the London Palladium company. One of the acts was an extremely witty comedian, Rod Hall and his emu. It was Hall's hand and arm that fashioned the head and neck of the emu; beneath his arm he carried the bird's "body". The bird was portrayed as a kind of rough-hewn bumpkin, coy, ingratiating, even loving when affection was lavished upon him; but he changed into a pugnacious, irascible fellow when he didn't like the turn of the conversation. The comic created this illusion with his own voice and his superb mime talents sketching the bird's personality. Naturally, I wanted Hall and his nutty bird to be my guest on "Luncheon Date." On the appointed day the comedian showed up with his sidekick tucked beneath his arm.

We exchanged pleasantries – how did Hall and the bird like Toronto, that kind of thing. Then, in the hope of pushing the bird into some truly inspired nonsense, I began attacking all birds in general, and this bird in particular. The comedian was superb; as my insults rained upon the bird's head he became increasingly agitated and annoyed. Finally, the emu was so enraged he attacked me, struck straight at my forehead with his bill. I was surprised and leaned away from the attack. My chair collapsed backward. The comedian, in a sincere effort to recover some decorum, lunged after me to prevent my upset. We ended up entangled together on our backs in the TV studio – one TV interviewer, one British comic and an emu. And the camera continued to roll. "What am I doing here?" indeed.

It's in the hope that I might, at least partially, answer that question that I am writing this book. I am not suggesting that Elwood Glover is a jet-set personality, a fit and proper subject for a biography. I can exist quite happily, secure in the knowledge that I'll never be cover boy for *Chatelaine*. Still, when a druggist in Halifax, a service station attendant in Sudbury, a waitress in Calgary and an on-duty policeman in Vancouver all recognize one's face, I think it is safe to say that one's "fame" is more than a purely local phenomenon.

This book is an attempt to explain how Elwood Glover and a TV program called "Luncheon Date" got together. I wrote the book for two reasons.

First, a lot of viewers who know me only as a fleeting face on their TV screens have asked how I got where I seem to be. (And this is as good a place as any to make a confession: Like most performers, I am blessed – or cursed – with a healthy ego. But . . . B U T, I am not so egotistical as to think that everyone who has seen "Luncheon Date" is holding his breath until I tell how I got started in broadcasting. Far from it. If you are one of those who couldn't care less about how Elwood Glover got started, take the book back and demand a refund. Tell them Elwood sent you.)

Second, I wanted to explain to *myself* how I got from there to here. I've knocked around in the broadcasting business – I almost wrote "racket" – for many years without consciously thinking of what my next step should be until after I had taken it. I wanted to pause, to "review the bidding," as bridge players say. A personal anecdote will set the scene.

My mother died in 1971 after a long and busy life that spanned ninety-two years. Among her last words to me was an admonition, some advice to an only child from a loving parent: "Now, Elwood, you look around and find something worthwhile and secure. You've been fooling around long enough."

Indeed I had. I was fifty-six years old when my mother voiced her last request. To that day I had never worked in anything but broadcasting; in her view I had spent thirty-five years "fooling around." Worse still, perhaps, was the fact that I didn't take my mother's deathbed advice but I don't think she would be angry. She was an eminently sensible woman who very early recognized that all of life is a choice between various options, options that change, shift and move about.

While I didn't take my mother's advice, I have never forgotten it. It is tucked into a fold of my brain very close to the surface; it pops up at the strangest times, while I'm driving, shaving and often when I was in the middle of a "Luncheon Date" interview. Whenever my ego is flowering or whenever my plans for the future are particularly grandiose, her words of caution come back ". . . worthwhile . . . secure . . . fooling around."

Like most Canadians of my generation I was raised to honor the puritan work ethic: "All work enobles; hard physical work enobles most." The thought that work, at which one earns a living, should also be fun is a heresy spawned in the sixties and seventies. My parents would have been shocked speechless to hear such blasphemy. My parents' moral code guided my childhood years; their prejudices became mine; my value judgments are made on a base established by my parents. To this day I often think, with the mantle of Victorian morals lying heavy on my shoulders, that the whole of the entertainment business is nothing but a lot of "fooling around."

Without being precious, this book is a kind of self-analysis in public. W. O. Mitchell, one of the best writers Canada has yet produced, once said that "writing is a private act until it's published." Like enjoying sex until you notice a voyeur peeking in the window. Writing, for me, is a traumatic experience and I am not at all sure I have reached any kind of a comfortable relationship with the task. For one thing, there's the permanence of a book. In radio and TV, every day starts with a slate wiped clean. But a book . . . it sits there accusingly. Sits there forever, never changing, while the author himself is bent, shaped, pushed, pulled and contorted into a dozen different new personalities.

Then, the critics. O, the critics.

It's difficult to escape the conclusion that critics see their function as an exercize in destruction. They take a hate on a particuar radio or TV show and set out to convince their readers to share their opinion.

I could go on for pages ranting about critics and criticism, but why waste your time and mine. In the course of this book, certain names will appear in context as critics; I thought of – and abandoned – the old melodramatic device of "(cheers)" for the heroes and "(hisses)" for the villains. I think my feelings about each will be obvious.

Well, critics be damned. This is *my* book about me and *my* program.

Back in 1915 there were no TV critics. Indeed there was no television. But there was, in the "wilds" of Saskatchewan near Moose Jaw, a little farming settlement called Carmel, and it was there on 11 May 1915 that I played to my first audience. In later life my mother told me that while my appearance left much to be desired, my voice was resonant

The back of this photograph carries these words: "Elwood Glover when he was a baby." Well, I'm not going to quarrel about that.

and carried well.

Carmel was eight miles north of Moose Jaw. My father's farm was a half-section (320 acres) of land south of George Lamb's place, and west of Jim Smith who owned more sections of land than I thought Saskatchewan contained. It was a good life for a child; the farm buildings were well kept, the crops were good, and the stock was vigorous and healthy. My father was a stern, austere man who had pioneered in the district. He knew at first hand the need for thrift and back-breaking work. Without doubt he was a good farmer but I didn't appreciate it at the time.

I learned to amuse myself; there were no near neighbors of my age. My cousins, children of my father's sisters, lived two miles to the north and west. They were my only – and infrequent – playmates. Curiously, I never thought of it as a lonely life. We had a foot-pedal pump organ in the parlor which was amusement for hours on end. Even more glamorous was the Edison gramophone that played wax cylinders; it sported a flowered, morning-glory horn suspended from a rod and chain and the cylinders were stored in blue, tubular containers. I luxuriated in the miracle of sound, songs like "Listen to the Mocking Bird" and "Snow Deer" sung by artists like Billy Murray and Ada Jones. With a child's simplistic view of the world I thought they sang for me alone. It never crossed my mind that hundreds, maybe thousands, of other people could hear "my" singers so mysteriously packaged on the grooved cylinders.

And there were animals – animals to play with, animals to care for. I had dogs, cats, baby chicks. There seemed always to be new pets, newly born or hatched. For a farm kid I was remarkably insulated from hard facts about "the birds and the bees." Sure, I knew that a cow was a cow and not a horse. But the physical means by which one horse created another (O, alright, *two* horses) was a question that never entered my mind. My first hint of sex came when I noticed in the Eaton's catalogue, the *Playboy* of my childhood, that men's winter underwear buttoned up the front but that women's didn't. That was a puzzler.

One day in early life I wandered into a local cemetery and noticed a tombstone that was incised, "Beloved wife

Three generations of Glover menfolk. I guess this was probably taken about 1919 when I was four.

and daughter of William J. A. Glover." My father's name.

It was an age when "children were seen but not heard." But this was a question of such moment that I broke the rule. And my question was answered, just barely. My mother was my father's second wife; his first wife and daughter had died several years before. I remember lying awake on my bed thinking that at one time I had a different mother and an older sister. As I grew in age and wisdom, I realized that the two deaths had bereaved my father but not me; my sorrow for my dad was great. Then, with still more maturity, I saw that but for the grace of God (or was it God's cruelty?) in taking my father's first wife, I might never have been born.

In 1920 when I was five my parents moved to the bustling town of Moose Jaw. The reason for the move tells a whole story about my childhood, my parents, their aspirations for me, their only child. We moved to Moose Jaw so I could be educated in a city school, the unspoken assumption being that an urban school was infinitely superior to the "little,

Nifty tailor I had when I was five. The trouble with "Sunday-best" — they never wore out, you outgrew them!

old, red schoolhouse." My father continued to work the farm; a married couple moved in as "hired hands" and dad commuted to work every day just like a 1970s suburbanite.

Moose Jaw's Alexandra Public School may have been superior to a country school – I never got a chance to make a comparison. But it certainly was a traumatic experience for Elwood Glover, aged five.

In the first place there were the swarms of noisy, pushy, city-sophisticated kids. It seemed to me that kindergarten alone was populated by 500 children. In the second place, my unsophisticated stance marked me as an outsider; on the first day of school, every other child in the school lined up to march into class. I strolled in by myself ignorantly unaware of the regimented protocol. Hoots of derision greeted my ignorance and my face flushed so red that I thought my ears would burn up and fall off. By the time class was dismissed the same afternoon, I had been well and truly marked as an outsider; the bully of the junior grades, a short, squat but muscular kid of about eight years, chased me home skipping small pebbles at my feet. A small gallery of fellow kindergarteners followed, cheering on the bully.

Another time (it may have been kindergarten or Grade One) the teacher told the class just before dismissing us that the following day each of us should bring a favorite toy and be prepared to tell the rest of the class *why* it was our favorite. I don't think I slept at all that night. What toy to take? What would I say to the class? I twisted sleeplessly in torment as these questions nagged at me.

The night finally passed and as the hour for school approached I finally settled on a small toy – a large toy would have made me too conspicuous – a tiny stuffed lamb on a wheeled platform with a long string for pulling. It was small enough to tuck into my pocket. The problem of what to say had not been resolved.

The first children to "Show-and-Tell," as contemporary teachers and pupils would call it, displayed their toys and with varying degrees of *savoir faire* carried off their little talks. Then, inevitably, it was my turn. I remember slinking to the front of the class trying to pull myself into a package no larger than my lamb. I extracted the small toy from my pocket, placed the wheels on the floor, picked up the string and started on my circuit of the classroom. At first the class was quiet but as I continued I heard a few giggles and snorts of amusement.

To this day I do not know what it was that prompted my next move; I stopped dead in my tracks, bent and picked up my lamb, and studied one of its four wheels with worried concern. For about thirty seconds I fiddled and twisted at the wheel all the while wearing what I hoped was an expression of grave consideration. In the time I was thus engaged with the toy, the undercurrent of giggles and snorting stopped entirely. I replaced the animal on the floor and concluded my trip about the room.

Every kid in the class was quiet when I started my talk. I told of how I met a poor, lost lamb while on my way home from school. Bleating for its mother, the poor creature was hungry, thirsty and frightened. One leg had been injured. I took the lamb home, fed it and gave it milk to drink. When it was feeling better I mended its leg and tried to find its mother. No avail. So the lamb continued to live with me and I continued to look after its leg; just a minute before, as I walked about the classroom, the lamb had complained of pain and I had stopped to ease it.

As I picked up the toy and prepared to return to my chair, I was stopped by a round of applause. It was several seconds before I realized that the applause was meant for me. *Me!* The bully's target and butt of innumerable childish cruelties. That applause, the spontaneous expression of acceptance by my peers, may have been the point at which my whole future was decided; certainly, I basked in good fellowship and learned in my own way, a maxim of the entertainment world: "A little bit of business always helps."

The episode with the injured lamb marked the end of my "school-is-hell" period. I did not immediately turn into a diligent scholar or become – hated words – a "teacher's pet." But the episode did reveal that the social context in which schooling is conducted need not be unpleasant. Instead of hostility, my classmates now greeted me with open arms as a welcome addition to their games; instead of being chased home by a bully's stones I walked home in

Every home had a family photograph propped up somewhere in the parlor. The prints were always rich sepia tones.

10

the company of friends.

The rest of public school passed pleasantly; I managed to scrape by on examinations without putting myself in any danger of winning scholarships or awards.

In the winter of 1927 – 8 I was taken to Chicago for an operation. From childhood I had been troubled with mal-

Not too young to dream, though. This snap was probably made when I was about thirteen on vacation at lake Manitou Saskatchewan.

functioning kidneys. My parents soon exhausted the Moose Jaw supply of specialists and upon local medical advice, I was taken to see a Chicago specialist. (Why I wasn't taken to the Mayo clinic at Rochester, Minnesota, I have never known.) The Chicago specialist diagnosed my kidney ailment as partially connected with a diseased appendix. So, in January 1928, I was bedridden in a small private hospital recuperating from surgery.

In the meantime, my father had retired from farming. He was forty-eight years old and was determined to enjoy himself in early retirement. As I had been plagued with kidney ailments, so had he been cursed with stomach trouble. Diet was always a concern. I was too young to know all the details at the time, but I imagine he consulted the same Chicago specialist who advised surgery. He never recovered from the anesthetic; we were told a blood clot was the cause of death. My mother took us home to Moose Jaw, me in the day coach, my father in his casket in the baggage car.

It was a dismal spring, 1928. I took longer to recover than was expected. Despondency coupled with slow recuperation kept me bedridden for several months. By the time I was well enough to return to school, it was too late to complete the term. My mother consulted with the principal and they decided I should return in the fall and repeat Grade Eight.

During my prolonged recuperation I spent hours thinking of the connection between my operation and my father's death. No matter how I shuffled the events it always turned out that had I not had *my* operation, my dad would still be living. It was a dreadful burden for a thirteen-year-old. It took years of slow maturing before I could see the whole episode with anything like objectivity.

High school was a breeze – not academically but socially. I was still an indifferent scholar, putting forth enough effort to get passing grades but no more. Socially I was in full bloom. The lesson learned with my lamb stayed me in good stead; not only was I accepted by my peers but, as often as not, was the ringleader in school clubs and casual escapades.

In the fall of 1932 I was seventeen years old and going into Grade Eleven. Over the previous summer I had, among other activities, spent a fair amount of time learning the fingering and technique of playing an alto saxophone. The instrument had been made famous by Rudy Vallee who was, for his time, a superstar created by the magic of radio. Any boy who played the sax was certain to be nicknamed "Rudy," a fate I somehow managed to escape. I learned to "play" the sax by following an instructional booklet that accompanied the instrument, supplemented with tips from a friend who also played sax. It was early evidenced that I would never be a world beater on the instrument; I could improvise fairly well but I couldn't "read" worth a damn.

When school started, I cornered friends, each of whom played an instrument, and we formed a dance band, "Elwood Glover and His Campus Boys." More than forty years later I can still remember each one of the group. In addition to the leader (me) on alto sax the group had a tenor sax, piano, drums and trumpet. We played for school "Lit" affairs, the social gatherings staged by the school's literary society, and as our fame spread (and it was spread pretty thin, I can tell you) we got invited to play for dances at the Oddfellows' Hall and the Orange Hall. We played in the basement of the Anglican Church for young people's every Tuesday night. But the most important engagement – important for Elwood Glover, that is – began with an encounter on Moose Jaw's main street. A gentleman I had known for a number of years, a man who had been my father's friend, stopped me on the street.

"Say, Elwood," he said, "I hear that dance band of your's is attracting quite a bit of attention. How would you like to do a show on the local radio station?" The gentleman was one of the guiding lights of Moose Jaw's one and only amateur station known by the call letters 10AB. (In later years when the station went commercial it was – and still is – known as CHAB.)

We discussed the details and as a result, every Monday 5:30 to 6:00 PM for several weeks during the fall and winter of 1932 – 3 "Elwood Glover and His Campus Boys" would pack their instruments down to the radio studio and fill in a half-hour's air time with our best arrangements. We shone with pride when a classmate said he had heard our show;

when an adult – a classmate's mother or a friend of my mother – mentioned he had heard the show we shimmered in the bright light of celebrity. It was a heady experience for seventeen- and eighteen-year-olds whose only contact with the musical world outside Moose Jaw came through late night, dance-band radio programs.

One Monday, we showed up at the studio to be told that the announcer who handled our show was ill and could not be present. We held a hurried consultation and decided to cancel the night's show. We *almost* decided. With perhaps fifty seconds left until air time, my drummer said, "Elwood, you know what we're going to play. Why don't you be the announcer?" With time pressing, it seemed like a sound proposition. The other guys in the band agreed and the operator, an amateur like us, agreed in the name of the station.

So it was on an early fall evening in 1932 in Moose Jaw, Saskatchewan, that Elwood Glover first let loose his dulcet tones on an unsuspecting radio audience. I wish I could say that I remember every historic word; I can't. No script survives. Even if we had had time to prepare a script we would not have done so. Radio was one hundred percent ad lib in those days although for a *really* important show we might scribble some notes on the back of an envelope. And "air checks," audio recordings, had not been introduced in those early days. So, the historic words have vanished forever (to which my tender ego mutters, "thank the good Lord for that small mercy").

In trying to re-create the past it seems to me that I should likely have been more proud of that performance than any other; after all, I had not only played lead sax and led the band, but "framed" the show, so to speak with my own voice. But re-creating the past is a dangerous business and I don't really think I was more – or less – proud of my spoken words than I was as a member of a five-man group. To be quite honest about it, I don't think I went to sleep that night with the thought that radio executives in Toronto or New York would soon be knocking on my door, let alone the bosses of CJRM or CKCK in Regina. Like every other person I knew, I was fascinated by radio; it bordered on the supernatural that a splayed wire playing over the exposed crystal face of a piece of quartz could pick up sounds made almost simultaneously dozens of miles away. *That* was the mystery, not the people who spoke the words. Just the fact that it happened! It was the miracle of the age.

The "Campus Boys" radio program was a limited engagement, limited largely by Mrs. Glover's belief that playing radio programs and other dance-band engagements kept her son, Elwood, from homework. She was undoubtedly right; the band – its engagements and rehearsals – kept me away from home about four nights out of the week. I had never been a natural scholar and that much time away from the books showed up rather plainly on my report cards. I folded the band and have not picked up an alto saxophone to this day. I *did* pick up my books though, and graduated from high school in June of 1933. At the time it was possible to take the first two years of a University of Saskatchewan arts course in Moose Jaw. I took the option. With second year university behind me I was still unsettled about my future. In spite of the gathering clouds that presaged the great depression of the thirties, it seemed to me that any young man should fasten his sights on business if he wanted a safe, stable future. It was with my mother's blessing that I entered a business college to equip myself for the world of finance. Almost at once I got part-time work in the office of a local insurance agency – not selling insurance but office work and typing. Right away it seemed that my judgment had been confirmed.

One day in 1935 my family friend, Carson Buchanan from CHAB, called and reminded me of the "Campus Boys" radio program. Was I still interested in radio and would I like to audition for an announcer's job? "Yes," resoundingly to both questions. At the appointed hour I took the audition and within a day I had another telephone call saying I had placed second in the audition behind a young man whose name I recognized.

What did the man who got the job have that I lacked? I asked the station manager. "The ability to sell commercial time," I was told and had to agree that I *was* deficient in that area. Indeed, I had never thought of the business side of radio as part of an announcer's job. I went back to business school during the day, my insurance work after school.

One year later, in 1936, almost a year to the very day, Carson Buchanan called again. Was I still interested in that radio job because the young man who got the job last year was moving on to a radio station in Regina. Again, "Yes!"

I started at the modest salary of twenty dollars monthly, a sum which I still insist was more a test of one's intention than representative of one's worth. (Within a year I was earning almost one hundred dollars monthly which tended to confirm my suspicion.) It was a fantastic learning situation. Greatest education in the world; everybody was new – including the audience. A performer could make a mistake without the audience jumping down his throat. We were free to make mistakes and learn from them. I opened the station door before 6:00 AM every day, cleaned up the studio and handled the 6:00 to 9:00 AM time period. From 9:00 AM until noon I was out on the street selling spots to local merchants and businessmen. From noon until about 3:00 PM I wrote the commercials and took them around to the

Fuzzy photograph of a young announcer at work. This was the CHAB *announcer's booth with the 250-watt transmitter in the background.*

advertisers for approval. Then, as often as not, I would return to the station in the evening to deliver the commercials I had written. (Some merchants were very choosy and wanted the man who sold the commercials to deliver them; there was no tape or disc recording equipment in those early days.) As I said, one would have to have been deaf, dumb and blind not to learn in that forced draught situation.

I took two week's vacation to the East in 1937 and armed with a letter of introduction sought out an announcer named Paul Luther at a Chicago station. Paul arranged for an audition at his own station, WBBM, and with a second station, WJJD, as well. At the second audition I was offered a job, on the spot, as a staff announcer starting at $125 *weekly*. I gulped hard and asked for a day to think it over. Twenty-four hours later I turned the offer down. I was scared out of my mind; what on earth, I thought, would a young guy from Moose Jaw do in a city like Chicago? Among other possibilities that occurred to me was that I'd be lost in no time – both figuratively *and* literally lost.

I returned home and I didn't mention the job offer to either my mother or my girlfriend.

I don't think I ever fully retained the overwhelming air of self-confidence that this 1937 portrait displays.

Sid Boyling of CHAB *coaches a nervous Elwood Glover who is about to start his first actuality broadcast at the Moose Jaw fair.*

The year was 1936 and I'd just been hired as a radio announcer, reason enough to put on the air of a suave sophisticate.

Violet Sharpe and her twin sister, Lillian, had been classmates of mine in Grade Twelve. Her parents and mine had been casual friends for years. Violet and I had seen a lot of each other in school but in the year before I had joined CHAB, we had both formed other alliances. We met again, informally, at the Moose Jaw fair of 1936 and took up where we had left off. Violet was in training as a nurse and very soon we had an understanding that when she graduated we would eventually be married.

My most exciting assignment at CHAB was to do a network program for the newly-formed CBC. It was to announce an "actuality" broadcast, a term coined to describe any program which originated outside a broadcast studio; with no recording equipment – actuality broadcasts were just that – actually happening at that very moment. The program was called "Night Shift" and was based on the premise that in a recovering economy, many industries worked around the clock to bring society its goods and services. "Night Shift" was intended to be a composite look at the men who work while most of us sleep. A single CBC operator (his name was Charlie Finlay) toured Western Canada putting the show on the network once every week with the help of local announcers. When it became Moose Jaw's turn, I was the one chosen for the crack at a national audience.

A few weeks after I did the "Night Shift" program, I received a letter from Gladstone Murray, who was the general manager of the CBC at the time. "Would Elwood Glover like to work for the CBC in Toronto?" the letter asked. My initial reaction was the same as when I received a job offer in Chicago: "No!" But, when I thought further about the letter I replied, "Yes, very interested. When do I start?" It was a giant step; I was moving from a small 500-watt station to a 50,000-watt key station of the new CBC network; it was an unheard of situation that had never happened before – or since. I was leaving the small rural atmosphere of Moose Jaw for the sophisticated *ambience* of Toronto. But on the positive side was an early entrée into the newly-formed CBC and the chance to grow with the corporation, to grow with Canada's radio.

It's March 1938 and V. Sharpe and E. Glover are engaged. The car, madame, is a '37 Pontiac hand-polished to a high lustre.

* * *

Before I sign off this chapter I want to say a few words about education. Rather, I want to say something about how my parents and their generation saw and thought about education.

Most Canadians of my generation were born to parents who had literally pioneered the country (as had my father) or who were but one short generation removed from pioneering stock. Education, to such pioneers, was more than the gateway to a fuller, finer life; it was a gold-sealed certificate that entitled the holder to escape the gut-busting labor of tilling the soil, of building graneries and barns, of hauling water, of pushing, pulling, cajolling some plot of bald prairie into a crop-bearing condition. In the early years of the twentieth century the back roads of every community fairly rang with the refrain, "No child of mine will have to work by the sweat of his brow."

I think that is a limited vision to bequeath to a child; indeed, if half the pioneers who uttered it were granted their wish, Canada today would be surfeited with theorizers and do-ers would be in short supply. Still, one can be in sympathy with the reason without approving the words in which it was phrased. Judging from my parents' actions I think the "No-child-of-mine . . ." phrase meant that education would provide for children an alternative. In my father's time a young man left school when he was able to wield a pitchfork, not when he turned a certain age. A child in those days assumed his only future lay on the farm or in the factory; "education" was something reserved for girls and sickly boys.

The more practical parents hoped that the end of education would be the establishment of the offspring in one of the professions which clearly did *not* require the expenditure of physical labor. Medicine was the most obvious outlet for a child whose parents were opposed to physical labor. "Become a lawyer . . . a banker . . . a bookkeeper . . . an accountant . . ." chanted parents right across this country. And a whole generation of Canadians, my generation, grew up believing that the be-all of life was "finding something worthwhile and secure."

As I have matured in time I have passed from being a son to being a husband, from being a husband to a husband-and-father. Finally I graduated to an even higher status as husband-father-grandfather. One thing that has impressed me during this metamorphosis is that many of us spend our time *un*learning those truisms of our childhood.

An incident that happened a few months ago really drove this message home. I received a letter from a nurse in a rest home for the aged in Winnipeg. The nurse had written at the request of an elderly patient, a bright-eyed eighty-year-old who watched "Luncheon Date" every day. The lady said, through her impromptu secretary, that the program was the central part of her day, that it formed the main part of her contact with the outside world.

I replied to the letter with "thank you" and little more. A few weeks later the nurse wrote back telling me that her elderly patient had died after "Luncheon Date" had signed off for the day. "The program was all that made her life worthwhile."

At last. I wish my mother could have read that letter. At last I *had* found something worthwhile. At last I had fulfilled my mother's last wish.

2

★★★★★★★★★★★★★★★★★★★★★★★★★★★★★

SOMEWHERE BACK THERE...

... I mentioned that as a boy I had been fascinated by the miracle of radio. Fascinated? I was goggle-eyed. For those youngsters in the audience who are too young to remember even pre-television days, let me try to recapture for you some of the magical aura that wrapped early radio.

As the nineteenth century glided downhill to its conclusion, two young men – one an American, one Italian – were tinkering away in workshops filled with complicated gadgets, most of them homemade. The American, Thomas Alva Edison, invented recordings in 1877 when he succeeded in putting his own voice onto a cylinder of wax. The gramophone that graced the front parlor of my home as a small child was a lineal descendant of Edison's first machine. Later (between 1879 and 1883) Edison invented the incandescent bulb which put inexpensive and automatic lighting into the cities and homes of almost the whole civilized world. In a larger sense Edison "invented" electricity in that he showed the world how to use electricity; without his daring first step we would not have today the stereo sound system, TV, mixmasters, toasters, hair dryers . . . the list is endless.

At about the same time, an Italian engineer and tinkerer named Guglielmo Marconi was fiddling around with radio waves in his attic laboratory in Bologna. Without connecting wires he was able to ring a bell in a distant room by pressing a button in his lab. Then, on 12 December 1901 Marconi floated a 400-foot antenna aloft of a kite over Signal Hill in St. John's, Newfoundland; in 1/86 of a second Marconi heard a pre-arranged reply signal broadcast from Cornwall, England, 2,170 miles distant.

When Marconi's radio was hooked up to "Edison's electricity," the result changed the world. But like most cataclysmic changes, it was slow and methodical.

The first radio receivers were crystal sets, simple gadgets in which a chunk of quartz crystal about the size of a walnut was the "receiver." Mounted on a base alongside the crystal was a piece of stiff, braided wire known as the "cat's whisker." Connected to the cat's whisker was a set of earphones, usually clamped hard about the ears of a radio nut. With a steady hand, the listener would probe the surface of the crystal with the cat's whisker. Certain parts of the crystal's surface would be vibrating in tune with the radio waves broadcast by near and distant stations. At this time, most – probably all – stations were run by amateurs. (Within years of radio's invention the governments of Canada, the United States and most nations of Europe were scrambling like mad to enact legislation controlling the use of the new device.)

By the time I was born, and certainly by the time I got interested in radio, crystal sets had been largely replaced by more sophisticated receivers using radio valves (tubes) and powered by wet or dry cell batteries.

I can remember distinctly the first radio I ever heard. It

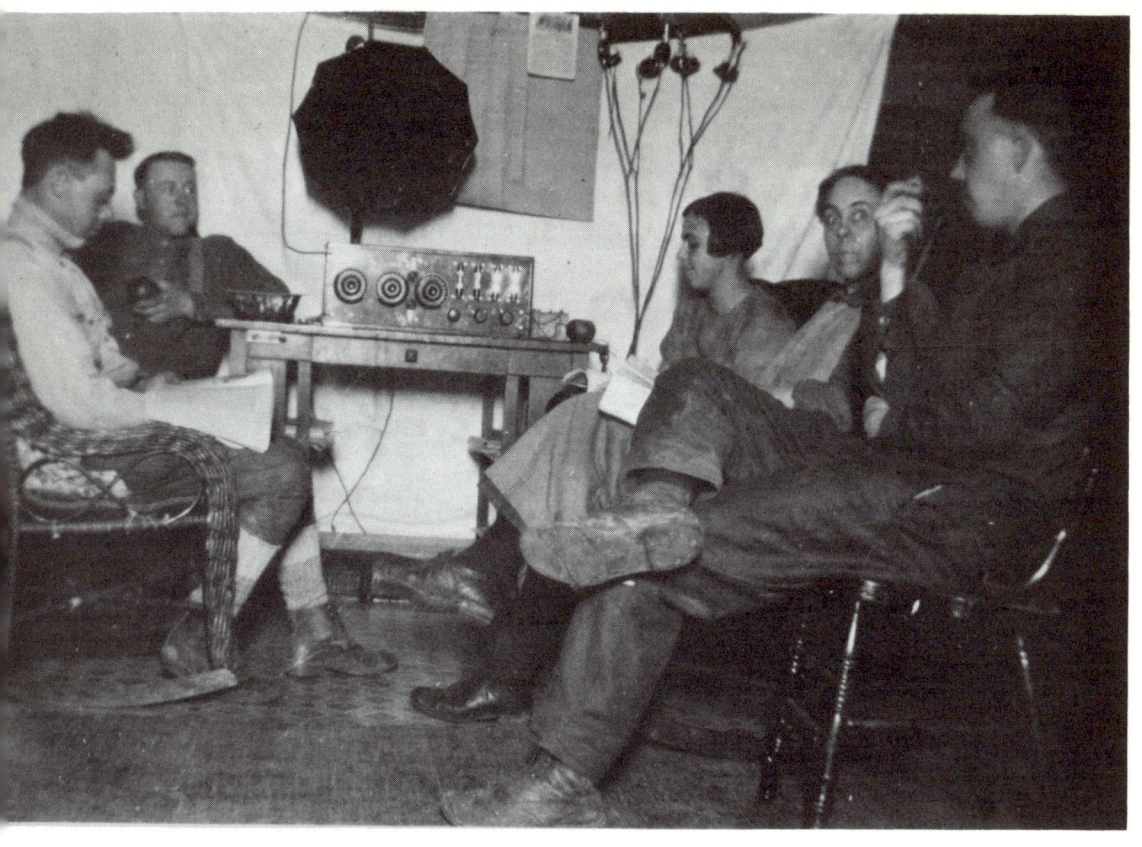

My cousins, the Grays, cluster around the first radio I ever heard. That's George in the foreground, left.

was a hot, muggy day in late summer and my father had driven me to the Gray farm to visit with my cousins. At one point in the evening's play, I became very thirsty and entered the house for a drink of water. My aunt was seated in a rocking chair beside a table on which rested a large, dark box, adorned with three large dials, each calibrated in minute gradations. Behind the box and connected to it was a large curved horn, about two feet high, looking like a giant's version of the ear trumpet some hard-of-hearing persons used. From the horn – mystery of mysteries! – issued the voice of a man. I was perplexed, confused, baffled. It was a trick, obviously, but how had my aunt accomplished it? Then, as I pondered this thought, the man's voice stopped and music – a piano, I remember – started. *That* was too much: My aunt didn't own a piano!

I demanded an explanation. A cousin, who had just entered the room, explained how it worked: George was a certified radio bug and was even building his own set. He explained how a gadget called a microphone picked up sound and fed it to a transmitter that converted the sound into another wave form that could travel great distances through the air. At the other end, a receiver like the one we were listening to, converted the radio waves back into sound waves we could hear. It was a revelation, a conversion.

As my father drove me home I asked him why we couldn't have a radio as my aunt and uncle had. My father was an austere and often stern man; but he was open in his affection for my mother and me even though he was spare in expressing his feelings. I don't recall his exact words but from what I know of him, I know he said something like, "It's a bit of foolishness made for man to waste his time." He did not – as did the parents of some of my friends – object to radio on religious ground; no "plaything of the Devil" from my father. Just a rock-ribbed opposition to anything that kept man from getting the job done. To this day I do not know how my father managed to twist his logic so as to permit an old gramophone and a pump organ in the house; I think they were likely concessions to my mother, an effete Easterner.

Having spoken once, my father considered it unnecessary to speak again. At odd moments I would chirp, "Sure wish we could have a radio," and he'd rumble, "I've told you why not."

So, throughout my childhood and early adolescence my radio listening was confined to what I could hear in the homes of friends. It would be self-slander to say that I chose my friends on the basis of whose parents owned a radio. Still, most of my friends of that era were so blessed, but it seemed to me that the Glover family was marked as rigidly resisting progress for its continued resistance to radio ownership.

When my father died in January 1928, I turned my constant plea on my mother. She, too, was a diligent parent but far less dogmatic about what constituted time-wasting gadgets and unnecessary luxuries. In a matter of months – indeed, I recall during my lengthy recuperation from the Chicago surgery – a large, shiny, walnut cabinet with a grilled front sat in a place of honor, beside the gramophone in our parlor.

Every day, for as long as I could wheedle, I would sit in front of the radio, my ear glued to the speaker grille, my right hand twiddling the station selector. (To my great amusement, my grandchildren refer to radio frequencies as "channels," the sure sign of a TV-age kid.) There was a real art to twiddling the dial – a heavy hand could obliterate five or six miniscule signals in a half-inch of dial. I often thought that a person who could sensitively tune a radio would make a good safecracker, like those experts in all of Jimmy Cagney's early movies who could feel the tumblers drop with the exquisitely sensitive tips of their fingers.

Luck played its part, too. This was early, *early* radio; the concept of network radio was just being discussed. What radio existed was just a bunch of amateur radio enthusiasts cranking out words for anyone who happened to be tuned to their frequency; radio was a motley group of low-powered stations grinding out grain prices and livestock quotations. There were no schedules – the station operators broadcast when they wanted to or, more likely, when their income-producing work was finished. There were few newscasts, few sports, no "Fibber McGee and Mollie," no soap operas, no radio at all, really, in the way in which the medium developed in the latter part of the twenties. Sure, some amateurs with more than the usual share of community goodwill would air items of local news: Whose baby was born. Who died. What eggs were selling for at the crossroads store. The scores of local lacrosse and baseball games. And even one benighted soul who I heard every afternoon at 5:30 over CKCK, Regina, who delighted in playing his favorite records for an audience he could only hope existed; had he but known, he had invented the job of the disc jockey some thirty years before the rest of the industry caught up with him. He should have patented the idea.

The frantic station twiddling that we early radio listeners engaged in was not for *what* we could hear but *how far* it came. "Hey," you'd say to the kid sitting beside you in math class the next day, "I got WLW Cincinnati last night!" He'd reply, "Yeah? Well *I* got KDKA, Pittsburgh, and it come in clear for at least a half-hour!" A bald-faced lie, concocted out of jealousy for your feat; Pittsburgh's signal faded so much by the time it reached Moose Jaw that you were lucky to hear even the identifying call letters.

It was magic, sheer magic, in those early days. Within an incredibly short period of time radio expanded, grew and changed. Much of the change was the visible result of pressure by government, both here and in the United States. But the rest was the result of a growing sophistication about the medium combined with a sharp eye on how profits might be maximized. The biggest change, from a listener's point of view, was the formation of networks feeding highly stylized programs to small, local stations. There was the Canadian Radio Commission for example, in Canada, feeding slick half-hour programs to CHAB in Moose Jaw, among dozens of others. There was NBC, CBS and the Mutual networks in the US.

(This is a good chance to pause and explain my theory about Western Canada: Every Eastern Canadian I know has, at one time or another, complained that the West seems to be more American than Canadian. Well, of course! Radio put into the hands of common, everyday Canadians, the most powerful medium of communication then known. While a listener in Moose Jaw, to take one example, might be able to pull in CKCK or CJRM, Regina, or CFQC, Saskatoon, he was literally flooded with several dozen stations broadcasting from the US – KFYR, Bismarck, North Dakota; WDAY, Fargo, North Dakota; KOA, Denver, Colorado; WCCO, Minneapolis and St. Paul; KFAB, Lincoln, Nebraska; and KPO from San Francisco; and KNX, Los Angeles. Take a look at a map of the West and you'll see that the central part of south Saskatchewan is located almost in the radio centre of North America.
It's not worth belaboring the point, but it surely is worthwhile to point out that in the early years of the twenties and thirties, the cultural barrage that engulfed Western Canada originated in the United States. Hardly surprising, then, that

Western Canadians are often assailed as American in outlook.)

With the networks came soap operas, those daily fifteen-minute chunks of life that gave us some peace from our own problems by concentrating on the problems of "Our Gal Sunday," "Ma Perkins," "Young Dr. Malone," and "Pepper Young's Family." Most of the soaps were broadcast daily; the outstanding exception was "One Man's Family," a half-hour weekly show that, for most of its incredible run on radio, played an early evening hour on Sunday and was heard in millions of homes from the Atlantic to the Pacific. If I close my eyes and concentrate, I can still hear the mellow voice of announcer Frank Barton as he opened the show: " 'One Man's Family' . . . a Carlton E. Morse production . . . dedicated to the younger generation and their bewildering offspring . . . Today, Chapter Nineteen, Book One Hundred and Seventeen . . ."

"Family" lasted on radio for two generations during which grandchildren were born and grew up, literally on the air. "Family" originated with a college drama group in San Francisco which later transferred to Los Angeles. And, in its own way, "One Man's Family" was a reflection of life in the unsettled days of the thirties. The protagonist was Father Barbour, a stockbroker, not wealthy but certainly comfortably well off. It must have been some cold comfort, at least, to millions of fans to hear that even with a modicum of income there were still personal and interpersonal problems arising in most families. "Vic and Sade" was another radio serial that achieved vast popularity. It concerned the everyday lives of a family of middle Americans and each episode began with the invitation, "It's early afternoon, halfway up in the next block." The scripts were literate and adult – the scripts assumed that you, the listener, were endowed with brains to think and reason with. I've often thought the "Vic and Sade" scripts could easily have been converted to novel form.

Another thing that network broadcasting brought along was commercials. O, sure, little local stations like CHAB in Moose Jaw, had been selling commercial spots to local merchants for some time; the networks brought in the big guns. To this day I still cannot hear of a certain brand of breakfast food without mentally identifying it as the "breakfast food of champions," that made, "Jack Armstrong, the All-American Boy."

The CBC was somewhat slower in filling the air time with money-producing commercials. When I first joined CBL in the spring of 1938, the only commercial I had to read was the "Twelve o'clock noon, B U L O V A, Bulova watch time" spot which was heard four or five times throughout the day – and that after the station had cut from the network and was broadcasting a local station break.

To keep the record straight I should say that at first, when networks began introducing commercial spots, I didn't appreciate their importance – their importance to me, that is. It was only after I became involved in broadcasting that I realized that commercials could help pay my salary. So important did commercials become that they were – and are – almost a necessary part of my life. In fact, my wedding day was planned around commercials I had to read.

When I first moved to the CBC in 1938 my fiancée, Violet, remained in Moose Jaw and continued her nurse's training at the hospital. As I settled into the routine of broadcasting from Toronto, and as Violet completed her training and worked for several months at a Regina hospital, it was decided that she would move to the East and become Mrs. Elwood Glover.

I'll never forget our wedding – nor do I think Violet will. It was planned around my commercials.

We were married at 5:00 PM on Friday 3 March 1939. The timing was crucial; between 4:15 and 4:30 I was required in the radio studio to deliver the commercials for the Crisco people on "Vic and Sade," and nothing, including my own wedding, could prevent me doing *that*. With luck the five o'clock wedding allowed us time enough to be married and still catch the New York Central train departing from Toronto's Union Station for Manhattan. We were treating ourselves to a whole weekend of honeymoon in the Big Apple. We had to return, however, early on Monday; I was scheduled to deliver the Proctor and Gamble commercials on "Pepper Young's Family" between 3:30 and 4:00 PM.

For two ecstatic days in Manhattan we spent every waking hour dashing from one radio studio to another. I had written ahead to all the networks asking for pairs of tickets; they were waiting for us at the Lexington Hotel. Among the shows I remember was a Sunday production of Fred Waring and his Pennsylvanians with Paul Douglas as the announcer. (Douglas later went on to a rewarding career as an actor in such movies as *The Solid Gold Cadillac*.) I'll never forget his appearance. There he was, the biggest of the big-time announcers, on a major Sunday program with the scruffiest, old pair of pants and sweat shirt I'd ever seen, with about four inches of bare legs showing before his feet terminated in tennis sneakers.

I was shocked – it was almost blasphemous! But then, on sober reflection, I began to see some advantages. Obviously, I had chosen well when I decided on a radio career; if Paul Douglas could rush from a weekend outing to introduce the Fred Waring program, surely Elwood Glover needn't be too concerned about his visual image – on radio, at any rate.

(It was a grand honeymoon – or so I thought for many years. In my mind it was only natural that Vi, as a new and starry-eyed bride, should have been thrilled to see all the radio celebrities in person. I guess it was with the rise of the feminist movement of recent years that I began to see the honeymoon for what it really was: the act of a thoughtless, male chauvinist prig who turned a honeymoon into a busman's holiday. If I haven't said it before, "Sorry, Vi.")

For two days Violet and I stuffed ourselves with radio – I can't remember if we even stopped for more appropriate nourishment. In forty-eight hours we must have seen and heard a dozen or more radio personalities who were supermen in my estimation.

In those early days who were my idols? That's a very easy question to answer. Since I began as a radio announcer in the mid-thirties, I have covered all fields of that profession through the radio years as a private station "do-everything-that-comes-your-way" type shows, "actuality" broadcasting,

In the last few years of "Luncheon Date's" existence I began hearing frequently from fans who had "passed your shop" or who "didn't realize you were a plumber." Finally, a fan who was also a photographer snapped this picture and cleared up the mystery. To the best of my knowledge the sign refers to a now-dissolved partnership to which a Mr. Elwood and a Mr. Glover gave their names. I tried, without success, to get the two men on the show. The sign, by the way, is located in Ithaca, New York.

to newscasting, to commercials. Through all these endeavors I was inspired by people I thought were *the* experts of their day.

I have to admit that my idols were, for the most part, American. When I started there was little to idolize in Canada. To take the sting out of that remark, I'll mention right now that Charles Jennings had the greatest radio voice that Canada ever produced; warm, vibrant, authoritative, with incredible projection; he was at his best when delivering the news or announcing a classical music program. Indeed, in the early days of the national news – broadcast coast to coast – Jennings *was* the voice of Canada. When he chose the executive route at the height of his career, it was Canadian radio's greatest loss. I had the pleasure, in the late forties, to work with Charles on the Symphony Pop Concerts from Massey Hall in Toronto every Friday night, sponsored by the Robert Simpson Company. How thrilled I was to work alongside a man I considered a living legend in this country. I could tell he loved being back in front of a microphone again – the same resonance, the same beautiful reading ability, the same dignity, it was all there.

We lost many of our great radio voices to administration or production in those days. John Kannawin, for example, who did the greatest actuality broadcast of its time – the collapse of the Rainbow Bridge at Niagara Falls in 1937. It was a masterpiece of word portraiture. And there was the late Ernest Morgan: His slight English accent didn't detract a bit from his lush baritone as he would enunciate "Samuel Hershenhorn and his orchestra."

J. Frank Willis, no matter how he tried, could never live down the fame the Moose River mine disaster brought him. A consumate performer, Frank Willis was equally adept at poetry and reading mood programs ("Atlantic Nocturne") as he was at describing historical events. T. O. Wiklund was a Dick MacDougal of his time, without the jazz-music affinity. He had an unbelievably dry sense of humor with the laconic, easy drawl Bing Crosby used to have. Wiklund had daring and was so cool. He had a fifteen-minute musical show with a singer named Sair Lee. He was outrageously funny, teasing the life out of her and breaking her up on several occasions. Nobody could get away with a sign-off like "this is the good old Canadian Broadcasting Corporation" like T. O. Wiklund could and not be called on the carpet for it.

My colleague in those early days, Herb May, I considered the greatest commercial announcer we ever had. Christopher Ellis of Montreal was another great voice.

An announcer perhaps no one will remember, but who had great style and personality, was Bob Freeland. I first heard him coming out of CJRC, Winnipeg, when I was still out West. What panache, what style.

Obviously, there were Canadians I liked and admired, but the big time was still the United States: NBC, CBS, the Mecca of the greats.

For actuality broadcasts, nobody could beat Bob Trout of CBS and George Hicks of NBC. In commercial announcing my favorites were Paul Douglas of CBS and Charles O'Connor of NBC (remember Johnny's "Call for Philip Morr-iss").

There was Don Hancock, Truman Bradley, Harlow Wilcox and Val Sherman – all graduates of WBBM Chicago.

In Hollywood there were the Niles brothers, Ken and Wendell, Art Gilmour, Don Wilson, Ken Carpenter (who always sounded like Don Wilson), Tom Hanlin of KNX who did all the Cocoanut Grove broadcasts. There was William Andrews and Cecil Underwood of San Francisco. It's funny, but Bill Goodwin of the old Bob Hope show never appealed to me. His was a higher voice and, in my mind in those days, the voice had to be rich and deep with an almost musical quality.

In the forties, before television started creating its own history, two radio personalities attracted my admiration more than any others. Both were American and they were similar in only two categories: they had an affinity for jazz and they both spoke on a high intellectual plane (or at least so it appeared to me). They were: Dave Garroway and Jean Shepherd.

Dave Garroway originated from WMAQ in Chicago with a late-night record show called "The 1160 Club" from 11:30 PM to 1:00 AM. Garroway was the ultimate in sophistication and intellect to me at the time. His style was low key and sprinkled with expressions like "iridescent" and "gossamer." He created a whole new world of ultra-cool which, before the rock scene came along with its screeching staccato, was one of the last gasps of fresh air radio ever breathed.

Jean Shepherd was a brilliant man whose gift was a photographic memory combined with the ability to talk without interruption from midnight to 5:00 AM. He got fired frequently and I was kept busy for years following him around the radio dial from WLW Cincinnati to KYW Philadelphia to WOR New York. Shepherd was exhausting, a compulsive talker who never stopped entertaining. I remember going to a Greenwich Village nightclub in New York in the late sixties. Jean Shepherd did his broadcast from a tiny stage surrounded by college students, from 10:30 until 12:00 P.M. He talked, he reminisced, cajoled, pricked pompous balloons in the social mores; in general he was a one-man life of the party for ninety minutes non-stop.

It saddens me to ponder the whereabouts of these two greats today. I understand they're still working, but a changing, cynical world has moved in and stifled their marvellous air of wonderment and imagination. Broadcasting is diminished by the loss of the magic these two men created.

In television the voice became less and less important. The visual medium overtook the audio because there were now faces to match up with the voices. The importance of sound dwindled to second place.

The aforementioned Garroway did well on television with eleven years of the "Today" show, his own "Garroway at Large" and the "Wide, Wide World" series.

Shepherd didn't make the transition. A few whimsical appearances and a travel series on educational television are the only contributions of which I know.

Television created a new set of idols — the talk-show hosts. I guess the first was Steve Allen, followed closely by Ernie Kovacs. They were the zanies of their time – products of the fifties. They were light and frivolous, usually counting on a sight gag as their main laugh-getter.

There was Jack Paar; a sharp wit and clever repartee were his chief assets. He had an unusual assortment of guests,

That's me (left) and Pa Cartwright sharing duties on a 1942 "Carry On, Canada" show. Pa's sometimes called Lorne Greene.

among them Dody Goodman, Genèvieve and Alexander King. Paar was brilliant at needling his guests and bringing out the ingredients for amusing conversation. Jack also brought psychoanalysis to television for the first time. His behavior was so unusual that the hobby of North America was to try to figure out "what is Jack Paar *really* like?"

Following Paar came the contemporaries – Mike Douglas, Merv Griffin and Johnny Carson and, for a while, Joey Bishop. The backgrounds of these four are interesting: two were ex-band singers, two were stand-up comedians. This indicated the developing phase of the talk-show host. In the earlier stages, those from radio made the best hosts because of their background in radio. Both Steve Allen and Jack Paar were radio announcers in their early careers. This stood them in good stead in the precarious role of talk-show host. Radio teaches you how to keep it rolling. Anybody who has worked in radio knows you mustn't leave dead air. The emergencies radio created were fraught with blank spaces that an alert radio announcer had to be prepared to fill at a

That's right: Duke Ellington and Elwood Glover having a drink together in Manhattan's Hurricane Club sometime in 1943.

moment's notice. This proved invaluable when hosting talk shows, proven time and time again when a comedian or stage or movie star would attempt to fill in. The technique must have panicked the majority of them because none that I know of ever made it.

Later, as time went on, singers and stand-up comedians seemed to fare better. Douglas, who was a singer with Kay Kayser's band, and Griffin, a singer with Freddie Martin, seemed to fit into the groove from the start, Griffin, not without considerable experience hosting game and quiz shows. Joey Bishop relies essentially on his comedy timing and dead-pan delivery which doesn't always stand up to the competition in the rivalry of the late-night time period. Whenever he replaces Johnny Carson on the "Tonight" show, though, he's much more comfortable, therefore funnier.

All this leaves Carson as the all-time supreme artist in this most critical field of television entertainment. He's the ultimate in TV personality projection. He has honed and perfected the ideal image of boyish rascality – cutting, razor-sharp wit and, above all making use of the medium (which can be fraught with error) to turn error or failure into humor itself. No one can surpass Carson when he's in trouble. No performer today has the ability to create utter disaster on a stage and not only survive it but put it to his own use.

Where does this leave Dick Cavett? That's the most difficult question raised by this subject because you really can't categorize Cavett. There is no question he is the most brilliant of them all, academically brighter than the rest, more erudite, more aware of the foibles of the world, more able to deal with the most abstract subject imaginable. He is also more daring in his choice of subjects and material.

So, you may well ask, why is Cavett at this point no longer with us? For the reasons I've mentioned – where Carson is the beloved clown, Cavett is more introverted, a more subtle wit, who, although he has the stiletto touch of a Groucho Marx, does not get through to the average North American who wants entertainment and movie stars along with his bottle of beer and chips. It is the rating race again. Dick Cavett was expendable.

Someone once drew an interesting analogy. If TV talk shows were considered as electronic magazines, Mike Douglas would be *Ladies Home Journal*; Merv Griffin would be *Cosmopolitan*; Johnny Carson would be *Playboy*; Dick Cavett would be the *New Yorker*. An apt comparison, I would say: Cavett is an acquired taste like caviar, olives and *New Yorker* prose.

Well, there they are – my favorite people in this profession. Idols? Yes. Influence? Maybe. Luckily, whatever can be said of my performance as a talk-show host, I was no imitator. I learned long ago that it is certain death in this profession to emulate another. But, I willingly admit these peers offered much in their deportment. What they taught

I was barely on staff when the CBC started to grind out this kind of publicity photo in 1938. The miracle of soft focus, make-up and touch-up!

me was showmanship, professionalism and audience relationship that I could have learned nowhere else.

What do I think is the ideal format for the current daytime talk show? The "Phil Donahue Show" from Chicago. It has all the ingredients of what day time audiences enjoy: big name stars, studio audience participation and phone-in comments from the viewers. (If only Phil Donahue would do something about that Merv Griffin-Mike Douglas hairdo!)

And speaking of appearances, I should tell you about my slightly absurd attempts to improve my own TV image. In the early fifties the leering eye of the TV camera began to look in my direction. One night, after a strenuous TV rehearsal, I heard a young director pontificate: "The television audience will never accept an announcer who wears glasses, has a moustache or who shows a receding hairline."

So intimidating was the new medium to me that I listened to those words with deep concern as if they had been graven on tablets of stone. I discarded my horn-rimmed glasses. (I needed them for close work only but I thought they added a note of serious concern to my somewhat puckish face.) I shaved off the pencil-thin moustache I had grown in idolatrous admiration of Ronald Coleman and Warner Baxter. Finally, I had some hairline fill-ins made specially in New York to compensate for a v-shaped forehead.

It's funny now; but twenty years ago with the Big Eye staring at me, it was all deadly serious. Had I but known of the mental pratfalls that TV had in store for me . . . well, I might at least have kept the moustache!

Photographs by Bruce Lowry

Anne Baxter

Anne Baxter has confused the Hollywood studio moguls for years; she won an Academy Award at the age of twenty three portraying a woman of forty. When she was fourteen she was hired to act the part of an eleven-year old in *Philadelphia Story*. (She was fired from this part – her blooming figure didn't look like an eleven-year old's.) Anne says the firing was the best thing that ever happened to her: "Acting is the supreme ego trip and it was good for me to have my ego punctured early." She goes on: "One of the best things of being an actress is that you're never satisfied. Sure, I was a star during Hollywood's star system But I was hard to categorize. I wasn't a glamor girl or a pin-up type, so they were never sure how to cast me. I confused them. Hollywood wasn't used to coping with an actress." Anne is the granddaughter of the famed American architect, Frank Lloyd Wright, and she lives by a tenet taught her by her grandfather: "See into life, don't just look at it."
(5 March 1975)

Virginia Payne

The radio soap opera of the thirties and forties captivated and influenced more people than any other form of communication. There was no more popular and enduring form of radio than the day-time serials. The most enduring of the soaps was "Ma Perkins" which lasted for twenty-seven years through 7,065 episodes. The star of the serial was Virginia Payne and when Miss Payne appeared in Toronto in a stage play, I *had* to meet her. On the "Luncheon Date" stage I asked her if the actors in the serial treated their roles seriously or did they deride and make fun of them. "O, we had fun," she said, "but not at the expense of the characters we portrayed. For one thing, we had only ninety minutes to rehearse *and* put the show on the air; you couldn't afford to clown around very much." At another place in this book I've mentioned my recurring nightmare; Miss Payne mentioned hers. "Because of the time difference between the East and the West coasts," she explained, "we had to do each 'Ma Perkins' show twice a day. Often, an actor would get into his car after the first broadcast and be halfway home before he realized he still had the second show to do. My dream always involves me as the only one of the actors left – there I am trying bravely to muddle through the script without any assistance whatsoever." Miss Payne told me the following story to indicate how the audience accepted the program as literally true. "At one point in the show," she said, "a little baby girl was left on Ma's doorstep. There was much discussion about whether Ma should keep the child. We received a letter from a gentleman in San Francisco saying that if we decided to give the child up, that he and his wife would give the baby a home. He wrote that he was retired, lived in a beautiful house overlooking the bay and that he and his wife would provide the baby with a happy, loving home. *And* he enclosed letters from his lawyer, his clergyman and his doctor as character witnesses." That was the power of radio; it will never happen again. Being part of that era I can readily believe that sort of thing happening. But I have recurring doubts about that lawyer, clergyman and doctor! *(29 December 1972)*

Chief Dan George

Chief Dan George personifies the Indian of our past that all of us have romanticized throughout our childhood. His stature, his roughly-hewn face – his is probably the most typical of all the Indian images any of us can recall. I think this endears him to the hearts of all who see him on stage, television or in the movies. He was seventy-five when this interview took place. He's a practical man and he's not impressed with the fact that he's now a movie star and celebrity. I asked him what he got out of this exciting business – does he like the glory and the fame? He said it was alright but, "I'm not in it for the fame or the glory or the honor: I'm in it for the money. I want to leave a little something substantial for my family after I pass on to the Happy Hunting Ground. That's my chief interest in the business." On the program, Chief Dan recited from his book of poetry, *My Heart Soars*. His dignity is immense and his soft voice was the perfect vehicle for his words.

O Great Spirit
Give me back the courage
　of the olden chief,
Let me wrestle with my
　surroundings,
Let me once again live in
　harmony
With my environment.
Let me humbly accept this
　new culture
And through it, rise up
　and go on.
Like the thunderbird of
　old
I shall rise again out of
　the sea.
I shall grab the instruments of the white
　man's success
His education, his skills,
And with his new tools
I shall build my race into
　the proudest segment of
　your society.
I shall see our young
　braves and our chiefs
Sitting in the house of law
　and government,
Ruling and being ruled by
　the knowledge and
　freedom
Of our great land.
(12 November 1974)

Wilfred Hyde-White

I cannot imagine Wilfred Hyde-White as a young man; in the dozens of roles he has played he has always been the upright, serious and precisely-spoken image of the grand old man. Only the twinkle in his eye gives him away. He told me that he became an actor because he was fascinated by the curtain calls taken by a troupe he had seen as a child. "It was just splendid to contemplate an audience, perhaps standing, perhaps cheering, as one took a bow at the footlights," he said. He used to practise taking curtain calls by regally descending the stairs at his home to the sound of imagined applause. "It was years before I realized that the curtain calls came only after three hours of hard work!" he recalled. "By that time I was too old to take up another craft." *(4 February 1975)*

Glenda Jackson

Glenda Jackson was probably one of the best interviews. Not *easy* – best. She is alert and nimble of mind; she expects to be fed questions with some meat on them and she responds with reasoned, well-thought-out answers. She answers the question completely – and then stops, waiting for the next question. An interview with Glenda Jackson is *not* a conversation; she makes the interviewer work. This was my second meeting with Miss Jackson (the first was in England during 1972) and at the second meeting she was gracious enough to recall with pleasure the first time we'd met. Naturally I was flattered and felt completely at ease with her. I'm often curious when interviewing people from the stage to detect if their manner of speech in conversation is as theatrical as their stage projection. Miss Jackson is very close to her stage delivery and I think this must spring from the English tradition of years of training in classical theatre. In other words, it rubs off in their everyday life. After the show an amusing incident occurred which demonstrates Miss Jackson's lack of ego.
Back in the dressing room I found her on the telephone trying to contact a number in England. The operator asked for details, as long-distance operators do, and when Miss Jackson was asked who was placing the call she said simply, "My name is Jackson." It would never occur to her that the fame of her name might have hurried up the call. A truly unpretentious woman.
(6 May 1975)

Tony Randall

It will come as no surprise to a fan of "The Odd Couple" to read that Tony Randall is a very funny man. His sharpest line on his "Luncheon Date" appearance occurred off camera. During a commercial break, I said to Tony, "You are interested in just about everything, aren't you?" To which he immediately snapped back: "Well, I've never tried buggery." The studio audience was convulsed. A few seconds before we went back on the air Tony whispered a challenge to me to repeat the question on the air. I don't usually take a dare but I couldn't resist this one; I repeated the question not knowing what to expect from the mercurial Mr. Randall. "Well," he replied, "I've never tried *buttery*." And followed up with a description of the big strong women who churned butter. The at-home audience must have wondered what on earth was so side-splittingly funny in *that* remark because the studio audience broke up a second time in shrieks of laughter at Tony's impudence. *(5 June 1975)*

Warren Beatty

Donald Sutherland

I don't know what to make of Warren Beatty. I admire him as an actor and as a film director. I recognize his *Bonnie and Clyde* as a landmark in the creativity of film. But in person there's a reckless, harum-scarum quality in Warren Beatty that prevents me from getting close to him. He's a notoriously bad interview. He seems to avoid taking anything seriously; I found myself sparring with him. At one point I asked him about the image he portrays in *Shampoo,* the image of a modern Don Juan, a womanizer. He stopped, gave me an "aw shucks" shrug and mumbled a reply that was no reply at all. I pressed him with another question semi-humorously dealing with his personal reputation as the answer to the prayers of any number of Hollywood women. He turned on me with a question of his own. "Are you married?" he wanted to know, an edge in his voice. Yes. "For how long?" he asked. "O, thirty-six years," I said. For a moment he stopped dead in his tracks; perhaps he expected a fellow Lothario and what was I doing probing about his personal life. He became very serious and launched into a homily about true love and continued devotion and how truly beautiful long-lasting relationships can be. It was touchingly said with humility and almost-yearning anxiety; the audience was completely captivated. I think I admired him more as an actor at that moment than ever before. But I still don't know quite what to make of Warren Beatty.
(10 March 1975)

It was on a movie set in Paris that I first met Donald Sutherland and found out to my happy surprise that he was an Elwood Glover fan from 'way back. Don was born in New Brunswick and was raised in Bridgewater, Nova Scotia. In his teens ("I was the youngest disc jockey in North America," he says) he ran a record show for a local CBC outlet and remembers listening to the network programs I had done. Don is, of course, one of the hottest stars in the movies today; he is also an active spokesman for many liberal-left causes and has been an ardent supporter of the activities of Jane Fonda. I wonder if Don's personal devotion to these causes may not waver a little as his success builds? Sutherland studied at the University of Toronto and got his start in acting on the campus. He recalls that he became mildly discouraged with his apparent lack of success as an actor. He decided to leave his future – acting or an alternative career – in the hands of a Toronto critic. If his next role was praised, he would be an actor; if it was panned, he'd look for other work. Fortunately for us the play was received with enthusiasm by the *Globe and Mail*'s critic, Herbert Whittaker. *(9 May 1975)*

Richard Todd

Everyone remembers the memorable role portrayed by Richard Todd of Peter Marshall in the film, *A Man Called Peter*. Peter Marshall had been a pastor and Todd so captured the dynamic force of the man that he is frequently stopped by persons on the street who recognize him and praise his style of preaching. "I've even been asked to address a Sunday congregation or two," Richard says. "I've even obliged on a few occasions; thank goodness I can remember enough lines from the film to give a convincing portrayal of a pastor who knows what he's doing." *(23 April 1975)*

Henry Fonda

Henry Fonda was seventy years old when I last interviewed him and he was touring in his remarkable one-man show based on the career of the brilliant lawyer, Clarence Darrow. I knew that Fonda had a history of heart trouble. "You wear a pacemaker, I understand," I said to him. "Funny," he replied, "I've never thought of it being worn." A pacemaker, of course, is a small electrical gadget implanted in the chest which stimulates the heart to beat regularly. Like any mechanical gadget, it must be supplied with some form of energy and so, several times a week, Fonda must sit still for a time while he gets himself recharged. To keep himself occupied while the recharging takes place you'll never guess what his hobby is – needlepoint. He's very good at it, too. *(28 April 1975)*

Robert Conrad

"Luncheon Date" made a potentially embarrassing mistake when Robert Conrad was my guest. I had been informed that *William* Conrad was to be on the show, William Conrad of the "Cannon" TV series. So pleased was I by this coup that for several days beforehand I announced that "Frank Cannon" would be our guest next Thursday. We didn't realize our error until the night before the show. What to do? I couldn't blurt out the truth in front of Robert and embarrass him; yet a studio full of Cannon fans – as well as viewers at home – would want to know where their idol was. Minutes before the show I thought of a solution; I went through the interview with Robert and a most affable guest he was. We discussed his roles in "Wild, Wild West" and "The Lawmen." At the conclusion of the interview I thanked him and he excused himself. During the commercial break I asked a member of the staff to let me know when Robert left the building and only then, explained to the audience the mistake we had made. Robert was spared the embarrassment and the audience had a plausible explanation for our mix-up. *Whewww . . .* It was a close one but such are the problems of live TV. *(15 May 1975)*

Beau Bridges

Beau Bridges is the son of actor Lloyd Bridges and, like other children of famous parents, lives somewhat in his father's shadow. But, his main problem, he told me, was that he is regularly sought to play the part of late teen-aged boys or of a youth in his early twenties. At the time of the interview Beau was already nearing thirty years so it's easy to appreciate his dilemma. He's concerned, I think, about the possible direction his career will take when he's thirty five or forty. "I am very conscious of time passing." he said. *(15 May 1975)*

Helen Hayes

I think I'd trade a day of my life just to spend an evening in the company of Helen Hayes. When she was my guest on "Luncheon Date" Miss Hayes was travelling to promote a Walt Disney movie. "What on earth are you – one of the best actresses in the world – doing in a Disney film?" I asked her. And her answer put life in its proper perspective. "There are two ways to grow old," she said. "You can be very depressing or very amusing. I choose the latter." I can remember the first movie Miss Hayes played in – *The Sin of Madelaine Claudet* which brought her her first Oscar. And, of course, another highlight of her film career was *Farewell to Arms* with Gary Cooper. Truly a fine actress, and a lady with a great philosophy: recognize the ability to grow old gracefully, and never fight its inevitability. She has earned her title honorably: The First Lady of the American Theatre. *(5 June 1975)*

Hume Cronyn Jessica Tandy

Carol Channing

One of the most astonishing bits of acting I have ever seen was performed by Hume Cronyn in the play, *Noel Coward in Two Keys*. In one scene, Cronyn was seated in a chair and confronted by two women who were blistering him with embarrassing questions. In the midst of the tirade Cronyn blushed, the most incredibly violent blush I have ever seen. I asked him how he managed this piece of stage business but he smiled secretly and waved the question aside. Cronyn and his wife, Jessica Tandy, have great love and respect for each other. They are devoted to the theatre and love talking about it. They don't necessarily agree with one another but they obviously enjoy testing ideas. Cronyn is the consummate actor, a finely finished professional. If one thing upsets him it is the "instant fame" that starring in a TV series confers on young and untried actors. He seems resentful that the star of a television series, a "star" who has not trained in the basics of stagecraft, can tour in summer stock and pack the theatres despite mediocre performances. This could be interpreted as jealousy of the box-office power of the television star but I don't think so. Hume Cronyn has a deep love for the theatre and it distresses him to see it It offends his passionate devotion to his craft.
(4 March 1975)

It's an exhilerating experience to be in Carol Channing's presence. She is larger than life on stage and, in person she is exactly the same. She looks at you with those saucer-like eyes, shakes her head of straw-coloured hair, gives you a wall-to-wall grin and talks with that husky, frog-like voice and exaggerated enunciation – I am convinced the Carol Channing on stage is the same Carol Channing off. She seems strangely isolated from the problems most people face; I've never heard of her being moody, depressed, "down," or disagreeable in any way. I once interviewed her on the set of a movie location in California, a movie the mercurial Otto Preminger was directing. Preminger's volatile temper was very much in evidence that day but Carol seemed totally unaffected by it; she listened to his tantrum with a look on her face as if she was a million miles away. I wouldn't be surprised if it were a defense mechanism. Carol's wide-eyed wonderment could very well be a buffer between her and the rough edges of show business. *(April 1793)*

Joan Fontaine

I cannot check on the actual date that Joan Fontaine appeared as my guest on the old radio version of "Luncheon Date." But, whenever it was, I had shortly beforehand seen her on Broadway in *Tea and Sympathy*. It was an exciting experience for me and I said so to Miss Fontaine. "That play was so sensitive and lovely and it was the first and only time I've ever played Broadway. The unknown young man who played opposite me went on to greater things – Tony Perkins." Miss Fontaine's sister is, as everyone knows, Olivia De Havilland. Miss Fontaine told me a story about Olivia that I'd never heard before: "I was at school in Japan and my sister had won a scholarship to a college in California. She was seen by a talent scout while she was playing in summer stock. She was signed to play the understudy to Hermia in *A Midsummer Night's Dream* and one of those unbelievable stage stories did take place: On the opening night the leading lady was ill. Olivia went on and captured not only the audience but all the reviews." Film buffs will know she subsequently played Hermia in Max Reinhardt's famed movie version. I asked Miss Fontaine who had been her favorite leading men in the long list of movies she had made: "Without a doubt, Charles Boyer and Ray Milland," she answered. But what was it like to work with [Sir] Lawrence Olivier in *Rebecca?* She hemmed and hawed for a second or two and then told me she'd answer *that* question after the show. She never did. She closed up as if the subject was something she did not wish to recall. Miss Fontaine's appearance was, as always, chic; she was beautifully dressed in a trim tailored navy suit with a white ruffled blouse and a wide brimmed, off the face, black straw hat which set off her blonde hair and flawless complexion. I can still recall the generous sprinkling of freckles across the bridge of her nose. Just another detail the Hollywood camera's soft-focus lens chooses to hide. *(1960-61?)*

John Payne

About 1941 or 42, there was a movie called *Sun Valley Serenade* that won my enthusiasm. It starred the Glenn Miller orchestra and an actor named John Payne who played the part of the Miller piano player. I'd seen Payne in lots of other pictures and at first he always seemed to play the "second banana," the rejected suitor or an unsympathetic "other man" in a triangular romance. Later he graduated to leading-man roles opposite such stars as Sonja Henie, Alice Faye and Gene Tierney. Payne doesn't seem to be too interested in the past; he wasn't too eager to talk about his acting career. Occasionally he's drawn back to the stage or screen but never, I think. for the adulation or applause of the crowds. He's made rather cynical remarks such as, "I thought I'd get back into acting to see if it's as big a rat race as it was when I was in it. It is." Payne was in Toronto with the tryout of *Good News,* a musical that had been adapted and directed by Abe Burrows; it was Payne's admiration of Burrows that led him to accept the part. He insisted that it was just a lark and at the end of the show's run he would return to his ranch in Montana and reclaim with relish his anonymity. I haven't heard or seen of John Payne for quite some time so I guess that's what he did. I think the near-fatal accident when he was hit by a car as he was crossing Madison Avenue at 61 Street in Manhattan in 1961 has made him appreciate the basic simplicity of life. He has no further illusions about fame and grandeur. *(22 January 1974)*

Colleen Moore

Colleen Moore is another star of the silent movie era who still looks precisely as she did when she was "gracing the silver screen." She wears the same boyish bobbed hair that became not only her own personal trademark but the symbol of the flapper era of the twenties. Miss Moore admits quite freely that she got into movies through influence. When she was a fifteen-year old and named Kathleen Morrison, she was given a screen test by the D. W. Griffith organization. Miss Moore's uncle was a Chicago newspaper editor who led the battle against censorship of Griffith's movie, *Intolerance*. The fight was successful and Griffith promised the editor anything he wanted – which turned out to be a screen test for his niece. She had help getting into movies but she survived and flourished with her own personality and talent. She not only appeared oblivious to the sordid side of Hollywood but rose above it all – though she did have a couple of unfortunate marriages. Today, widowed, she is part of a socially prominent Chicago family and reflects fondly on her former movie-star role. She has no illusions or wish to resume that part of her life. *(23 February 1968)*

Peter Ustinov

What can I say about Peter Ustinov? He's an actor, a recording star, a playwright, a director, a notable success in all his careers. Most of all he is a brilliant wit. He's a big man physically and mentally his intellect is immense. On Peter's appearance on "Luncheon Date" we talked of many things but most of his comments were on the pressures of late twentieth-century life. "I don't know what we have to look forward to" he said. "The man who designed the first airplane to fly the English Channel is still alive and lucid in his nineties in France. He is still alive in the year in which the Americans have reached the moon. It's uncanny the progress we have made since 1900; transport, communications, science – we've added far more knowledge about all these things since 1900 than through all of history before. Our means of communication are fantastic but man hasn't invented anything new to say to himself. I find that frightening." Peter's appearance was just a few days before Christmas and after the show the "Luncheon Date" crew was adjourning to a hotel suite for a holiday party. I hesitatingly asked Peter if he would join us, allowing him to decline gracefully. He said he was delighted to be asked and later, when I had to leave to get back to another assignment, I said goodbye and he remarked, "O, how sad. I was just beginning to enjoy myself." *(22 December 1969)*

Eartha Kitt

Eartha Kitt was one of the first guests to appear on the TV version of "Luncheon Date." It's so long ago that I don't really remember what we talked about but she was at the peak of her popularity. She'd been a cast member of *New Faces,* the Broadway revue, and had cut a few records that were selling well and she was a Broadway star. Shortly after she had been in Toronto I saw Eartha in a play in New York and I went backstage to tell her how much I had enjoyed her acting. Now, going backstage is not a favourite pastime of mine; actors are usually drained after a performance and they want and need some solitude to unwind, so I usually respect their wishes. But on this occasion I made an exception. I was shown into Eartha's dressing room and she was seated at her makeup table. We conversed – if you can call it that – through the mirror! She remained facing the mirror the whole time and talked to my mirrored image. I watched and talked to *her* face in the mirror. Not once did she turn and talk to me directly. It was like writing a letter to a friend and sending it through a third person. Eartha was was not being rude or temperamental; she was just that tense after coming off stage. It was a long time before I ever went backstage again. *(early-1960s)*

Lorne Greene

Whenever Lorne Greene appeared on "Luncheon Date" it was more like a meeting of old friends than an interview. Lorne and I have known each other since the early forties when he arrived at CBC Toronto from Ottawa. Even then we all knew he was destined

for the big time. His voice was deeply resonant – the CBC staff announcers had a standing joke that Greene and Alan MacFee, would have resonance contests and when Greene won (as he always seemed to) MacFee would burn the studio! Lorne was assigned to the national news during those terrible days of the early war years so it was perhaps natural that he should be dubbed "The Voice of Doom." The country literally came to a halt each night when the news was on. In addition to the marvellous instrument that was his voice, Greene had an unquenchable dramatic flair. (He later put this talent to great use as a dramatic actor on stage and screen, culminating in one of the best loved television character of all time – Pa Cartwright in "Bonanza.") Sometimes CBC management thought Lorne put too much drama into the news. No such thing! The drama was already there. It took a Lorne Greene with his sonorous sound to bring home the impact of the horror of war. *(29 October 1974)*

51

Margaret Hamilton

The name of Margaret Hamilton may not ring an immediate bell in the minds of film fans. Miss Hamilton is one of those solid professionals whose roles in movies and plays provide a background against which the better-known stars can shine. As a result, while you recognize her face, you seldom remember her name. Her most famous role was that of the "Wicked Witch of the West" in *The Wizard of Oz*. Among several movies prior to that I remember her most for a secondary role in *My Little Chickadee*, the W. C. Fields-Mae West romp. I once met Miss Hamilton in Houston, Texas, where I'd gone to tape a series of interviews on the set of a movie in the famous Astrodome. She was appearing in a stage play in that city and was cast for a part in this movie which was called *Brewster McLeod*. She saved the trip for me; the starring actors, brash newcomers all, (and where are they today?) couldn't have cared less about being interviewed and had no interest in publicity. Miss Hamilton was the embodiement of graciousness. Even she was aware of their indifference and shrugged rather sadly at the comparison of their attitude to young actors of the past. After her last appearance on "Luncheon Date" I received a letter (which is very rare in this business) in which her warm generosity comes through: "I have finally decided," she wrote, "that the reason I would rather be interviewed by you more than anyone else in the country (this or any other country) is that you have such great taste before [the interview] and on the air. You make me feel really so welcome . . . your questions are considerate and kind and encouraging – not probing!" A warm, friendly woman of the old school is Margaret Hamilton. Speaking of stars who respond following talk-show appearances there are a few who do take the trouble. Joan Crawford rigidly follows this ritual, and does it immediately. Others who make a point of this are Charleton Heston, Arthur Godfrey, Jerry Lewis, Rudy Vallee and Kathryn (Mrs. Bing) Crosby. *(18 April 1974)*

Melvyn Douglas

I sat down with Melvyn Douglas in the dining room of the Four Seasons Hotel when "Luncheon Date," still in its infancy, was a radio show. Douglas was in town for a taping of a television drama by Bernard Slade titled *A Very Close Family*. The film *Hud* had just opened and the name Melvyn Douglas was being heralded far and wide as an Academy Award possibility in 1963. His 1939 film, *Ninotchka,* with Greta Garbo was a triumph for Douglas as well as Garbo. Naturally the subject came up: What was Garbo really like? Douglas said, "All the stories and legends about Garbo were true, but often distorted in the telling. Garbo hated giving interviews to the press and, of course, the story got around that she loathed publicity. Not at all. She did not dislike the press and she knew the importance of publicity. She was just extremely shy." Douglas said that on the set of their third picture together she ordered screens placed so she would be hidden from the gaze of her fellow actors during close-ups. I asked him about what we all assume were the "great years" of Hollywood; the star system, the contract player, and would these days ever come back. "I doubt they would," he said without hesitation "and in my opinion that's by no means a tragedy. We're better off without that particular era." I asked him what he found wrong with it. "If you wanted to work in Hollywood you signed what I used to call a 'baseball players' contract. It gave the studio total control over you and your name and left you as an actor with no say in your

own affairs. If you were the least bit adventurous about your career as an actor, it was stifling." Douglas revealed he'd been a Toronto resident in his early life. His father was associated with the Conservatory of Music. "Yes, I lived here from about 1910 to 1915," he said. "In fact, I was sitting in the audience at the old Shea's theatre watching a vaudeville performance when World War I was declared. I wasn't in show business then – I was quite content to watch from the other side of the footlights." He must have been about twelve years old then. I told Douglas that I, for one, would be happy to consider him a Toronto alumnus – "I don't think Mary Pickford and Walter Huston should have all the glory." Douglas chuckled as he accepted the compliment.
(10 June 1963)

Yul Brynner

Yul Brynner is every bit as imposing in person as he is on the stage or on the screen. He is polite, agreeable and submits most graciously to being interviewed. He is a man of great dignity. Brynner was born on a Siberian island called Sakhalin and his real name is Taidje Khan Jr. I suspect Brynner is capable of great anger so I resisted the desire to ask him what must be the most often-repeated question in his life: "Why do you shave your head?" I don't think I could have survived the flint-like glint in his eyes or the tightening of the jaw muscles. Or what would have been worse – his walking off stage (which I understand has happened).
(27 February 1975)

Gloria Swanson

She is the personification of the living legend – Gloria Swanson is seventy six and one of the most glamorous women the screen ever revealed. Her complexion is flawless and her secret of longevity, she says, is health food. Indeed, so fanatic is she about diet that the whole "Luncheon Date" interview was given over to the subject; she showed no desire to reminisce about her movie roles. Her vitality is immense and, by her own admission, she is wildly extravagant – she earned eight million dollars in eight years and spent every cent of it. "My epitaph should read, 'She paid all her bills'," she said. Her philosophy is, "Life is ninety-five percent anticipation, five percent realization; learn to live with anticipation – it's more fun than achievement."
(30 March 1971)

Ted Knight

Ted Baxter, the big, stereotyped simpleton of a newscaster on the "Mary Tyler Moore" show, is merely a role for Ted Knight to play. In real life, Ted is a bright and sharp conversationalist, as far removed from the pompous Baxter character as possible. Ted told me that the Ted Baxter character developed as a routine with which

53

he amused his friends; when he was asked to audition for the Moore show, he read some lines as Baxter and . . . well, a whole new life developed. Ted Knight's real name will surprise you: Tadeusz Wladziu Konopka. I will vouch for the spelling, never for the pronounciation! *(June 1973)*

Wendy Hiller

She is one of the best actresses to have come out of the English theatre which is reason enough to include Wendy Hiller in this book. There's another reason as well; after her appearance on "Luncheon Date" (the first time she'd granted a request for a TV interview) Miss Hiller offered to help me get an interview in London with Dame Sybil Thorndike. For almost one year Miss Hiller and I corresponded and, through her good graces, I was able to tape an interview with Dame Sybil the following year, an interview the viewers and I will never forget. I have been forever grateful for her promise fulfilled.

Readers with long memories may remember Miss Hiller as the definitive Eliza Doolittle in *Pygmalion,* a role for which George Bernard Shaw personally selected her. More recently she starred as Queen Mother Mary in *Crown Matrimonial,* a stunningly realistic performance in the drama about the abdication of Edward VIII. It was my privilege to see the show on opening night and the memory of Miss Hiller's lofty dignity will remain with me forever. It was on that occasion that Wendy Hiller told me the delightful news that Dame Sybil would be pleased to do the interview if we could come to her home. We did and I hope you saw the result. *(7 August 1972)*

Gina Lollabridgida

'Way back in 1962 the news got around that Gina Lollobrigida, her husband and young son were to move to Toronto. The house was picked out and for years after, the street was crowded as Torontonians and tourists drove past to see Gina's house; she and her family lived there for one week! Eleven years later on the "Luncheon Date" show Gina was in town promoting her book of photography, *Italia Mia.* She photographed Italy's places and people for years and had accumulated more than 20,000 pictures before she decided to publish. The most difficult job of all was not taking the pictures although she went for hours, even days, for just the right shot. It was the agonized task of narrowing the choice down to 191. She produced the whole book; she chose the paper to be used and the size of the page, she supervised the lithography, executed the design, chose the binding and used her own diary notes as text. I asked her if she didn't collect galleries of on-lookers wherever she worked – after all, how often does one see a glamorous movie star playing photographer. She told me how she masqueraded in formless old clothes, a fright wig, horn-rimmed glasses and carried two plum pits tucked into her cheeks. An unrecognizable picture of one of the world's most beautiful women as she "holds up" the Tower of Pisa is the book's final photograph. It may come as a surprise to you men out there: Gina's eyes are her most beautiful feature (limpid as the eyes of a doe). *(3 December 1973)*

Douglas Fairbanks Jr.

As a "Luncheon Date" guest, Douglas Fairbanks Jr. was a very quiet, suave, rather thin, middle-aged man – the personification of ultra-conservatism. Fairbank's two visits to the program were highlights for me because his father had been one of my early movie heroes. I had grown up with Doug Sr. from the early days of the silent era through the advent of the talking picture. "Swashbuckler" was a word invented to describe Douglas Fairbanks Sr. Douglas Jr. resembles his father considerably but was more often cast in drawing-room comedies and idle-rich roles. But he has a versatility and charm that have made him as much a movie star as his father before him. He could "swashbuckle" with the best of them as was evident in one of his best pictures, *The Corsican Brothers*. One of the things about Fairbanks is you can watch him today in a movie made in the early thirties and you are not embarrassed by the overacting that many stars of that time could not overcome. If you ever get a chance to see the original *Dawn Patrol*, you'll see he was much more believable than his two co-stars. He was always sincere in each part he played, acted without superfluous frills with great personal magnetism.
(5 December 1974)

Virginia Mayo

I looked forward to meeting Virginia Mayo. I wasn't exactly a fan but I admired her as a beautiful showgirl from the days of the Goldwyn musicals and had always found her an acceptable leading lady opposite such stars as Danny Kaye, Burt Lancaster and Gregory Peck in *The Secret Life of Walter Mitty, The Flame and the Arrow,* and *Captain Horatio Hornblower.* Since the usual arrangement with the public relations representative of the Royal Alexandra Theatre was to bring leading players to the program I was quite pleased when I heard that Virginia Mayo would be on the next day. When she arrived I knew I was in trouble. I was introduced and I received a rather diffident "hello" to which the PR man behind her shrugged indicating to me right away that I was in for a bad time. Now, I should explain that a few celebrities hate TV interviews. They resent that their privacy has to be interrupted at ungodly hours in order to "hype" the publicity of whatever vehicle they're appearing in. Sometimes it's in their contract, sometimes it's necessary if a frantic theatre management sees that the advance isn't too good or the box office isn't doing enough business. In any case, my sympathy is usually with these people so I try to be especially polite and courteous in order to make them feel welcome. Miss Mayo was not happy. She sat down by herself in the lobby of the Four Seasons showing impatience and discontent. When she came over to my desk, for the interview her answer to my opening question was curt. I wondered what in the world was bothering her. You can tell when a woman is disturbed when she answers a question with a question. I'd ask, "How did the show go last night?" She shrugged, "How do you think it went?" "Do you enjoy stage work after making so many movies?" "What's to enjoy?" Then she'd notice her image in the monitor and start primping. "O, look at my hair. Doesn't it look awful?" she'd say. I thought I'd try something different: "Of all the leading men you've worked with (Greg Peck, James Cagney, Gordon MacRae, Danny Kaye) who were the best to get along with?" "They were all the same," she shrugged again. "Now that you're on the stage, do you prefer light comedy parts or would you rather do heavy drama?" "Is there a choice?" I think I recall asking her, ". . . if you had a choice, Miss Mayo, where would you rather be right now?" expecting her to say ". . . anywhere but here." Instead I got, "Who knows?" I finally gave up, thanked her, went to commercial and prepared for the next guest. I often wondered what was wrong with her. Being so uncooperative and uncommunicative why would she consent to appear? For that matter if touring was that annoying why would she go out on the road and endure the inconveniences?

Then I began to wonder if she were that withdrawn all the time. Maybe she has a feeling that she has nothing to offer on interview programs and she covers her insecurity with a studied indifference. This is the worst thought: Does she feel that having been a famous movie actress at one time that it's demeaning to travel in mediocre stage plays (I don't recall the reviews being too good) or is it an inner rage that finds expression in a resentment of everything in general? (Perhaps age in particular?) The finish of this incident is even more bewildering. Several months later she was in Toronto in another play at the Royal Alexandra and guess who came up to the Four Seasons for another appearance on "Luncheon Date?" Virginia Mayo. What happened? Same thing. *(1965-6?)*

Alfred Hitchcock

How do you handle a guest whose favorite practical joke is to say to a friend in a crowded elevator: "I didn't think one shot could make such a mess, did you? There was blood everywhere." Such is the whimsical humor of Alfred Hitchcock. The same sense of humor places him in at least one scene in each of his movies. (The most ingenious: *Lifeboat* where there wasn't even room for another passenger, let alone someone as recognizable as Hitchcock. Solution: a photograph on a soggy scrap of newspaper.) Scenes from several Hitchcock movies are for me forever memorable: The imperturbable Robert Donat as he marched undaunted in a street parade while escaping as a fugitive (*39 Steps*), the mysterious finger-drawn message on the steamy window of a railway coach (*The Lady Vanishes*), a film based entirely on a single scene, an apartment courtyard framed as if on a proscenium stage (*Rear Window*), the sight of that ugly gothic house in the murky dusk (*Psycho*). His film, *Topaz,* had just been released at the time of my interview with Hitchcock, and I asked him why he'd chosen a story so wrapped up in political overtones (an unusual premise for a Hitchcock picture). "The politics of *Topaz* is just window dressing" he answered. "When you get, for example, a spy story and you say to yourself what are the spies after? It doesn't really matter what they're after. It matters to the characters in the movie but not to the audience. The public doesn't care about the 'papers,' or the 'plans' or the 'fort.' It's the suspense regarding them that matters."

Hitchcock told me about making *Notorious* in which the plot revolved around the discovery of uranium. "A year before Hiroshima we made that picture," he said, "and I wanted to show what these cunning Nazis were up to in South America. Ben Hecht, the writer and I visited a scientist. We asked what size an atom bomb would be and how it would work. He spent an hour telling us the whole thing was impossible. Well, we made the movie anyway and I was later told that I'd been shadowed by the FBI for three months. They figured I was trying to sell atomic secrets." I asked Hitchcock about the famous Cary Grant scene in *North by Northwest* in which Grant is pursued across the open prairie by a crop-dusting airplane. "That scene was done in that way to avoid falling into the usual cliché," he said. "Here was a situation in which a man is to be put on the spot. The typical scene would call for a darkened street, an eerie street light, cobbles washed with a recent rain, a face would peer from a window and a black cat would slither by. That's the cliché. I tried to imagine a scene as far removed from that cliché as possible. Bright sunshine, no houses, no trees, nowhere to hide. Being chased by a plane over flat fields created its own form of terror." We talked about fear and his use of this emotion in his movies. He illustrated an example with a remark about *Psycho* – "It was made with a sense of amusement on my part. It was rather like taking the audience through the haunted house in the neighborhood. It amuses me to watch people being shocked as much as it amuses them to be shocked." As a final question I asked Hitchcock why fear was such an important thing in his life, he seemed to dwell on it constantly. He said, "We all have fears. We've had them since we were babies. Our mothers threatened us with the 'bogeyman' if we didn't behave. Later, we began to enjoy fear – we went on a swing, we went higher and higher to scare ourselves. Later, we paid money to go into the 'haunted house' at the fairgrounds." Alfred Hitchcock creates fear for the vicarious enjoyment of the public. Incidentally, he vehemently denies that he ever made the comment that all actors are cattle. What he really said was "all actors should be treated like cattle!" He looked straight ahead without a trace of a twinkle. *(9 December 1969)*

Keir Dullea

Keir (rhymes with "peer") Dullea (pronounced "deLay") is, with the exception of George Hamilton IV, the most pro-Canadian American I've ever met. For a number of months he and his family lived in Toronto and even today Keir says he plans to take out citizenship. I first became aware of Keir when he played a moody, introverted young man in one of the truly good American art films, *David and Lisa*. Sometime later he became the human foil for the computer, Hal, in Stanley Kubrick's *2001: A Space Odyssey*. Since that landmark film he has appeared in a number of pictures and television plays – a surprisingly large percentage of them either made in Canada or co-starring Canadian actors; he starred on Broadway, for instance, in the revival of *Cat on a Hot Tin Roof* with Kate Reid. At the time of this interview Keir was involved in publicity for his latest film, *Paperback Hero,* in which he plays a Western Canadian hockey star who dreams of glory as a modern re-creation of a gunslinging lawman. In my opinion, this is one of the best Canadian films yet made. It's an accurate portrayal of how a lot of young Western Canadians live (I'm *not* talking about the tragic ending), in fantasy created by American popular culture. *(17 March 1975)*

3

★★★★★★★★★★★★★★★★★★★★★★★★★★★★★

THE RUMORS SWIRLED...

... around the city: "TV announcer poisoned on television," "Elwood Glover rushed to hospital with arsenic poisoning," "TV client picks shoddy way of removing pitchman for product." The rumors were, thank goodness, just that. But they illustrate the frightening ease with which television can create and destroy.

It was on a TV program under the label of "variety" that was produced live every Monday evening called "Mr. Showbusiness." It was based on the reminiscences of Jack Arthur, a performer and producer whose career spanned at least thirty-five years in Canadian entertainment. He was a master showman of his day, that day spanning everything

Jack Arthur

from the early days of vaudeville to running the grandstand show at the Canadian National Exhibition. It was a TV program that included a huge twenty-piece orchestra conducted by Howard Cable, a chorus of dancers directed by Alan Lund and such performers as Alfie Scopp, Ben

Lennick, Sammy Sales, Johnny Moreland, Doreen Hume, Joyce Sullivan, Terry Dale and Wally Koster. It was all done live from the CBC's Studio 4 on Yonge Street which Alex Barris once labelled lovingly as a book title, *The Pierce Arrow Showroom Is Leaking.* It was a cavernous area, huge as a barn, and was able to accommodate all the equipment necessary for black-and-white television plus a large stage area with a bleachers section for a studio audience. These were the days before videotape, chroma-key and instant playback. There was no such thing as a second studio for commercial production. When a dance routine concluded, four stage hands went into frantic action. Two wrestled a long table into position when the dancers had vacated the floor. A backdrop descended from the rafters. A third stage hand placed four dishes of ice cream on the table. The fourth stage hand sprayed three of the four dishes of ice cream with Fly-tox to keep the flies, encouraged and warmed by the heat of the lights, off the ice cream. The fourth dish was left unsprayed for the announcer – me – to eat as he murmured, "Mmmmm . . . that's good." The whole operation was rehearsed and re-rehearsed until it could be performed in less than ten seconds.

During an actual performance one fateful night the producer watched the dance number conclude on his monitor. Allowing the pause for the scene change he signalled the camera to pick up the face of Elwood Glover intent on extolling the virtues of the sponsor's ice cream. As I came to the end of the spiel, I picked up a spoon, plunged it into the dish of ice cream, and lifted it to my mouth. Before I bit down I knew something was wrong; the ice cream smelled acrid, medicinal. In a micro-second I knew what had happened: *My* dish of ice cream had been sprayed along with the others. There came, as it must to all men, a moment of decision. I had three options. First I could refuse to take the bite in which case my "Mmmmm . . . that's good" line would have to be abandoned. Second, I could take the bite, turn my back and spit it out (an unthinkable breach of TV etiquette) hoping the client wouldn't sue. Third, I could swallow the ice cream and carry on as if nothing had happened and let the fly spray eat at my innards. There was no choice, really, I *had* to continue. I took the bite, swallowed hard, composed my face into a look of ecstatic delight, smacked my lips and murmured, "Mmmmm . . . that's good." Now, if that had been the final utterance I might have got away with it, but I had six more lines to say and I couldn't exactly mumble words of ecstatic pleasure with a mouthful of runny ice cream. So down it went with a feeling of bravery over and beyond the call of duty, giving my all, even my life, for a dearly beloved sponsor. My fifty-nine seconds of horror were over. The camera's red light went out, the table was whisked from sight and the show's action continued without interuption. I slumped to a chair, damp with perspiration. It was small consolation that a scientifically-minded stage hand calculated that I would have had to swallow three *cans* of fly spray before the poison content would begin to affect me. I should hasten to add that a huge dinner following the show, which I later gave up in the middle of the night, eased my anxiety and also my life span. Next morning I was happy to be around so I could reiterate Mark Twain's famous line, "Reports of my passing are greatly exaggerated."

All sorts of crazy things happened on "Mr. Showbusiness." Like the double they once hired to pour some milk into a container. For some reason they couldn't get a close-up of me doing it so they had this actor hired and all he had to do was pour a carton of milk into a pitcher with a pair of the most nervous hands even seen on television. He shook like he was a Dr. Jekyll preparing for Mr. Hyde. So the criticism the next day was, "Hey, how come you were nervous last night on that commercial. What happened?"

The inside word among staffers who manned television shows was that every performer who needed a cue card or a teleprompter was an idiot. In fact, that's how the name originated – "idiot cards." It was a damaging, ego-deflater to anyone with years of radio experience to be termed mentally deficient because suddenly you were expected to memorize everything you said on camera. Radio was the last experience in the world that taught you to expand your memory. In radio, if you didn't ad lib, you read everything. You spent years learning to "lift it off the paper" and suddenly there was no paper to lift from. Nor should there be any in the eyes of all the amateur experts behind the scenes. You could see the shrug of disapproval as a stage hand would be assigned to print up and hold a cue card for a nervous and insecure performer. "You dumb cluck," you could almost hear them saying under their breath. "Look at that jerk, he probably has trouble remembering his name and address." And the trouble was, even with cue cards or a teleprompter, there's a definite technique to using them. You need practice; it's not easy to use these and still make the TV audience unaware of their use. Even today, how many times do you see the eyes wavering off to the side or above the lens as the performer is extolling the merits of your favorite soap flakes or shampoo? And there's nothing more disconcerting to a viewer, either; it's like somebody talking to you while looking past your right ear. That was the trouble back then; there was no time to practise, no chance to mark the script as we used to do in radio. I used to plead with producers to leave me alone for a few minutes while I ran through the card copy or the prompter roll, even marking them with a felt pencil when necessary, just to get the feel of the lines so you could at least lift a few of them off the paper and put them directly into the lens. But no, it was never possible. No time. No cameraman. No cue card holder or teleprompter operator. Besides, they were on their break and weren't due back until show time.

Before I tell you about my first TV show, let me tell you about the most nerve-wracking experience I ever had. It left me devastated, drained and feeling hopelessly incompetent.

Robin Hood Flour Mills had retained me for many years as their radio spokesman for the Claire Wallace "They Tell Me" program and for its successor, the "Musical Kitchen" show. It starred Howard Cable's orchestra, Terry Dale, Bernard Johnson, and June Dennis as Rita Martin, cooking consultant. As the fifties emerged radio was in its death throes commercially; all the big commercial shows were feeling the threat of oblivion – Borden's "Canadian Cavalcade," Pond's "John and Judy," the "Northern Electric Hour" – all except the "Happy Gang" and Wayne and Shuster who clung to the radio network like spiders waiting for their web to be swept away.

The Robin Hood people decided on acquiring the Canadian rights to the current heart throb of American television, Liberace. And, so it was decided that I was to be their spokesman on television as well as on radio.

Came the day for the taping of the commercial inserts and everybody from the client to the agency with their entire retinue were on hand to see that this "giant step for mankind" was taken with the greatest efficiency and with the benefit of all their combined expertise. Naturally, the focus of their attention was on me in the centre of Studio 2 where I was supposed to come prepared with opening and closing announcements and two one-minute commercials all timed and ready to deliver live to be inserted into the American program. The tension I spoke about a few paragraphs back was nothing compared to this ghastly occasion of trying to repeat with total recall what I had spent many tortuous hours memorizing the night before with the added hazard of changes that had to be made at the last minute in the script as well as timing to the split second to be right on the dot for the cut-in's allotted time.

Now, I must tell you that the wizard of the Canadian commercial television field at that time was Joel Aldred. He was the phenomenon of the age. As well as his imposing presence and his deep resonant voice, he had a photographic memory. He could whiz through his Westinghouse commercials with the experience of an American. Of course, what everybody knew, was that Aldred (as a johnny-come-lately to radio) whizzed through everything he did with infuriating aplomb and a confidence that rivaled that of General George Patton. Aldred was simply a natural with blazing ambition and colossal nerve (and I mean that as a compliment). He knew the right people and was absolutely without fear.

I remember when he first joined the staff at the CBC in the mid-forties. I took him aside, as older pros are wont to do, and said, "Joel, you've got a lot on the ball, I think you're going to go places. You're new in this business, so let me give you a little personal advice. That first name of yours has got to go; it's too hard for the listener to make out, too many vowel sounds, it's too big a mouthful. Why don't you change it, why don't you shorten it to Jay Aldred? It's got a nice ring, it's easy to remember and you'll sound like a big time American announcer." Well, the next thing I knew, he was using it. He used it for several days on his morning radio show. I felt great pride when I heard, ringing loud and clear, "This is Jay Aldred speaking, CBL Toronto." Then suddenly it stopped and he was back to Joel Aldred. I never knew why and I never thought to ask him.

But, I was right about one thing. He *was* big time American before many months had passed. It was the Aldred image that everybody else in the business had to be compared to. He was the example that very few could touch, and my trouble was I could feel the aura of comparison as I stood there under those lights struggling through those Robin Hood commercials enduring dozens of retakes with my nerves becoming threadbare as time dragged on.

The ultimate humiliation was when the agency, which was paying for all this overtime, had to suggest that during the supper break they'd write out all the lines on cards. Then we'd go over to Spence Caldwell's office which was across the street on Jarvis, and rehearse my feeble ability to get the material off the paper. I was almost hysterical because as well as feeling completely incompetent all this was taking place in front of my old radio-agency associates who had worked with me in the past. They had a respect for my ability and were confidence boosters right down the line. That was the monstrous experience of my first TV commercial. Luckily, after a few Liberace shows, and with practice at home on how to handle the reading of idiot cards, I began to feel less like one and was able to complete the Liberace series without incident.

Teleprompters, however, were something else. One teleprompter operator (who is still around the CBC, in what capacity I don't know) had great difficulty in rolling the machine to my pace of reading. With no time for extra rehearsal, for his benefit or mine, we went on the air. We got through the first commercial alright. The second was where it happened. First he had trouble with the switch so that it would stop and start erratically through the first thirty

A few minutes to air time and I'm studying my script – the back of an envelope. Undated, the snap is probably post-1939.

seconds of the spiel. Then, the final disaster, the copy roll simply left its container above the lens and rolled down across the floor like a roll of toilet paper ending up under the stands of the studio audience. This is the final outrage. With a panic that overcomes you when you realize you are now on your own and you've got to get out of this, in frantic desperation you ad lib what remains of the message trying to make sense while you're mentally counting off the remaining seconds praying that you'll come out at fifty-nine seconds on the nose – with all this calamity, something tells you inside that this is no way to live. This is the final debacle that makes you glad you never left radio. I remember the commercial producer, Dave Thomas, coming down out of the booth after the show and confirming what I had already decided; sticking to radio was a good idea for the remainder of 1954 and into the early summer of 1955. Luckily, memories fade fast and time heals a multitude of wounds in this crazy business.

An actor who learns a new role in a short period of time is said to be a "quick study." Due to the protective arm of radio, and never being an actor on stage, I had not acquired the skill of a retentive memory. Therefore I began to write off television as a medium beyond the possibility of mastering. Nurtured so long by the unseen communication of voice alone, I resigned myself to accept the fact that the visual amenities of temple fill-ins, the removal of a moustache

and the abandonment of spectacles were just not enough to
enhance the visual presence of Elwood Glover and make him
presentable to the public. I felt that from the very beginning
television was trying to tell me something and I was slow in
getting the message.

Perhaps I should tell you about my first exposure to TV
which occurred in the summer of 1952, long before "Mr.
Showbusiness" came along, when I was called to replace an
ailing Dick MacDougal. It was a Saturday-night jazz show
featuring Trump Davidson's Dixieland Band and
assorted singers. The setting was a radio disc jockey show
but with the music provided from a live band. It was complete with a small announcer's booth, a control board with
a desk, microphone, two turntables and real records. The
announcer – on this particular night, me – was to introduce
the recording, make a show of cueing the record and then
throw an imaginary switch that would bring in the Davidson
band with the music. The idea was to emulate what a real DJ
does. Things went swimmingly, until, during one of my most
verbose and ornate introductions, a section of the backdrop
to the set broke away from its moorings and began hurtling
towards the turntable. I caught this out of the corner of my
eye, reaching up in time to catch its downward plunge and
can you imagine the scene? Here's a guy trying to cue a
record, letting go of the turntable arm which immediately
ran wild across the grooves of the record cutting them up
unmercifully, holding up a piece of scenery while uttering
some banal remark like, "Well, folks, you know how it is . . .
something new every minute. Due to circumstances beyond
our control we have a slight problem here."

I remember I was rather pleased with myself for not
blowing my cool; I'd saved the show, probably, with my
calmly delivered lines. If this was the worst that could happen
in television, I thought, maybe the old radio savvy could get
me through any situation.

At the conclusion of the show, the producer rushed down
from his booth and headed straight for me, his face wreathed
in smiles. I thought, "Ah, he's going to congratulate me for
saving his show." But he went streaking past me to embrace
a lighting man who had achieved some spectacular effect the

producer was particularly fond of and evidently had come off.

There was nothing for it but to gather up my sense of bravery, nurse my bruised ego and leave for home. Come to think of it, that producer may have known more than I did. Perhaps in that lighting man he could spot genius when all I saw was competence. As a matter of fact that director went on to greater things in TV and movies; you may recall his name, Norman Jewison.

Wounds heal, scars of humiliation dissipate, time obliterates the memories and by the summer of 1955 I had more or less recovered from the icy bath in which television had plunged me. Jackie Rae, who had directed the "Mr. Showbusiness" series I've already mentioned, had moved on to become Director of Variety for CBC-TV. He asked me to write and emcee a half-hour of prime time on Saturday night to be called "Jazz With Jackson" which was to star the talented America-born pianist, Calvin Jackson, with Peter Appleyard who had just arrived from England. Jim Guthro was to be the producer. It was an easy-going show, relaxed and informal. I shall always be grateful to Jackie Rae for having faith in me and to Jim Guthro for his confidence and patience because "Jazz With Jackson" proved to be such a happy show that my confidence returned and for the first time I found I could face the one-eyed monster and survive its relentless, nerveless stare. It also provided me with my first experience as a TV interviewer.

I could go on for pages about television's persistent intent to humiliate me, but for a strange reason the nightmares I still have are all based on the horrors of radio – missed cues, losing my place in a script, being late for a broadcast, sight reading and freezing at misplaced punctuation.

A traumatic occurrence took place during the forties when I was assigned to emcee a series of Victory Loan Broadcasts. These shows, bolstered with Hollywood's biggest names, promoted the sale of Victory Bonds through which part of Canada's war effort was financed. Stars like Greer Garson, Ronald Coleman, Walter Pidgeon, Ingrid Bergman, Brian Aherne, Shirley Temple, Yvonne de Carlo willingly gave of their time and came up to Canada at the invitation of the Canadian government.

Partially hidden behind the microphones is Glenn Miller, in London, Ontario, for a one-night stand and we're on the air for the Mutual network.

The shows were broadcast from Toronto's Massey Hall with Percy Faith's full orchestra on stage and I remember Austin Willis, Lorne Greene and Jack Dennett were prominently featured in this series. I recall how I had to resurrect the old tuxedo I had purchased years before (when I did the "Music by Faith" series from the old Margaret Eaton Hall at McGill and Yonge Streets) and had a tailor re-locate the buttons so I could close the jacket over what was my rapidly expanding middle. My God was I nervous when I realized I had the responsibility of this prestigious series which involved audience warm-up as well as the on-air show.

On the night of the program I walked out on the stage and began to chat with the audience, the idea being to put them into a relaxed frame of mind, telling them when to applaud and when not to, telling them about the split-second timing involved, generally getting the audience on the performers' side. It was a good crowd, ready to respond. As air time approached I sought out my lectern, a small stand to hold my script, and told the audience that when we were on the air the house lights would be extinguished but just watch me, I'd signal when I wanted applause.

Well, the house lights dimmed as I expected but on my lectern there was total darkness. It was pitch black with not even spill-over light from the musicians' stands to illuminate my script. I muttered a short prayer and, with eyes closed, launched into my opening remarks which ran almost a full minute in length. My prayer must have been heard; from memory alone I re-created the introduction, kept the guest stars' names straight, didn't stumble over my own tongue. When I checked later I found I hadn't strayed more than a few words from the script, a feat I couldn't repeat even if I'd memorized it. During the first musical number a stage hand found me an extra music stand complete *with* light; my let-out dinner jacket was soaking wet and I felt it shrinking even tighter as panic and its reaction tortured me through to the end.

That Victory Loan Broadcast has remained to haunt my dreams. The situation recurs in altered form, sometimes; my script will be totally blank or I'm trying to read it upside down. Most of the time, though, I find myself trapped in front of an open mike without enough light to see the typescript. That episode happened more than thirty years ago and it's strange that radio, the simpler medium, is what haunts me, not television. I won't philosophize about it, but it certainly says something about the human mind that an incident that happened that long ago still has the power to pull me, hysterical, out of deep sleep several times a year.

Still, it seemed to me that radio was infinitely more gentle on a performer than was television. Most shows – with the exception of studio-audience shows, symphony broadcasts, variety programs and sports – were put on the air by two people: the announcer and his operator or technician. The announcer paid attention to his operator's hand signals and that was the end of it. In the early days of television there seemed to be at least ten or twenty people each one assuming he had the right to guide and instruct the man on which the camera was focussed. I can remember so many moments

During a 1946 jazz concert at Toronto's Massey Hall this collection of Toronto disc jockeys posed for an intermission photograph. From the left: Keith Sandy, Stu Kenny, Michael Wood, Wally Crouter, singer Phyllis Marshall, Bill Kemp, Larry Mann, Elwood Glover. In front: Dick MacDougal and Ben Langbord, record-store owner.

of panic in the control room and on the floor, that it seemed a miracle that any shows were done at all, let alone done well!

The 1940s produced a curious phenomenon in the United States, the personality disc jockey. This could be anyone from a staff announcer who could ad lib (what the public would call 'the gift of gab' and the critics referred to as the 'gift of gaffe'). Or, as developed, a field of employment for unemployed band leaders – the big-band profession was rapidly drawing to a close. The disc jockey became a new and fearful influence in the recording business. This occurred partly because of the depletion of expensive, big-budget shows leaving blocks of program time to be filled; and because of a burgeoning recording industry. The greatest promotion medium possible fell into the hands of the record makers with the advent of the disc jockey. They were the new élite. Primarily they fed off the industry that supported them. Pioneers like Al Jarvis, Martin Block, Allan Freed, Bill Randall of Cleveland, Eddie Gallagher of Washington and Howard Miller of Chicago took on a stature that was nigh on dictatorial. How bewildering in the eyes of a reasonably intelligent public that Phase 2 of the profession of radio announcing (a catalystic profession at best) should suddenly become a power of influence and a molder of taste. At least four of these record spinners showed a modicum of talent and went on to become entertainers in their own right, namely Arthur Godfrey, Steve Allen, Jack Paar and Dave Garroway.

But for the most part, the disc jockey became a feared and favored member of the entertainment industry. And as a result the balloon of importance inflated to such a degree that in the 1950s it burst with a governmental investigation into the payoff scandal. Let me hastily say that much of this investigation never involved Canada. Not necessarily because of our lily-white purity or shock that such a thing might even be contemplated; it was simply a matter of economics – Canada's record industry at that time was so minimal that collusion of this kind was not advantageous. Certainly Canada had its record-company representatives and naturally they were friendly to disc jockeys who got to meet all the big stars and were invited to cocktail parties. But payoffs? I never heard of one. An occasional bottle of liquor at Christmas as a friendly "thank you" was the usual gesture and that would be from a record representative who was a personal friend. But under-the-counter remuneration, as far as I knew, was non-existent. There wasn't the dog-eat-dog competition among disc jockeys in Canada. There was no fighting for the privilege of releasing potential hits first that there was in the United States. There was never the back-biting, cloak-and-dagger maneuvering that our American friends endured. In the late forties and early fifties we all had genuine respect for each other and enjoyed trading quips in each other's company. In Toronto this was the great age of disc-jockey conviviality: Keith Sandy, Joe Crysdale, Mickey Lester and Stu Kenny at CKEY; Harvey Dobbs, Monty Hall, Dick MacDougal and Larry Mann at CHUM; Barry Nesbitt, Phil McKellar and George Raymond at CKFH; Wally Crouter, Bill Deegan, Earl Warren of CFRB. (All of whom are still intact at RB, incidentally.) But I digress.

At CJBC at that time there was a freelance DJ during the supper-hour period called Michael Wood who was, believe it or not, a student of mine in an announcing class I conducted at Ryerson Institute of Technology in 1947. Come to think of it that was quite a roster during that class of 1947-8: Howard Cooney, John Grenfell of CBC Montreal, Bill Knapp, CHCH, Hamilton, and Michael Wood among many others that I've lost track of.

Wood was an exceptional performer in a day when every DJ tried to be more unctuous than the other. It was the era

Violet and Elwood Glover at a broacasting-industry awards dinner in 1947 where I was voted by Radio World as Canada's most popular announcer. It paid to be with Claire Wallace following the "Happy Gang." Hugh Bartlett won the year before.

of the soft sell, of contrived intimacy. Everyone with a radio voice sought a sound, a distinctive style, that would set him apart from anybody else. It was a phase that radio went through following World War II. Up till then, BDJ (before disc jockeys), radio announcing depended on four things – a good projective voice; good diction; the ability not to stutter; and to lift the material off the paper. The DJ changed all that. The voice need not be round and mellifluous; in fact, the quieter you could talk the better. You had to get "inside" your audience, make each listener, he or she, think that they were the only person in the world that you were talking to. (Sometimes I thought that's all there was.) It was cozy, manipulative, seductive. Dave Garroway's greeting, "Hello there, old Tiger, and you with the hole in your head," or words similar, that was the age of the one-sided conversation with an audience in which the technique was "never give them a chance to answer back even under their breath."

Michael Wood did a program called "Off the Record" which leaned on jazz, mostly, from 4:30 until 7:00 PM and he was the epitome of what I used to call "crotch talk." There wasn't a housewife within earshot of Michael Wood's dulcet tones that didn't experience an immediate disdain of every obnoxious quality her husband ever had. Funny thing about Michael: I can hear his style as if it were still on the air today but I can't recall one thing he actually said. The effect was the thing. The image he created – that was the essence.

I consider this period of CJBC's English-language era as the peak of its listener appeal. Bruce Smith in the morning, Byng Whitteker in the late AM, Al Maitland in the early afternoon, John Rae with an hour of classical music, Cy Mack and, later, Austin Willis with an hour of talk and music. Then, Michael Wood.

I remember during my "Musically Yours" days on the network, envying him his utter abandon to vocal seduction, something I never thought I was able to master although I heard from some that I came close. Time as it comes to all men, from the magazine of the same name, moves inevitably onward and Michael Wood was off to better things. Why I could never understand; he never had it so good in the brief

The lady is Claire Wallace, whose radio program, "They Tell Me," was an immensely popular attraction for listeners as witness her mail. I was also the mailman.

few years he was a broadcaster although I'm sure he would argue that today. He is at present the manager of the Saskatchewan Centre of the Arts in Regina. However, I recall that his departure for parts unknown left the station in a dilemma. "Where will we find his likes again?" I could hear them saying with much wringing of hands.

The station manager, Bob Kesten, and his assistant, Bob McGall, recalled the success of "Musically Yours" which I had concluded in June of 1949 and they asked if I'd temporarily sit in for the vacated period of "Off the Record." I jumped at the chance. Perhaps I should explain the demise of "Musically Yours" which really was just a departure; the program continued for many years from Montreal where its title was changed and it remained for at least a decade longer.

The pressure at that time was rather horrendous in those early afternoon hours. I'd been working with Claire Wallace since 1943 on her regular "They Tell Me" series following the "Happy Gang" and working with this delightful lady with no responsibility as to content meant that I could do Claire's show and "Musically Yours" with relative ease there being a half-hour in between. But at the completion of Claire Wallace's contract near the end of the forties and with me taking on a new, live, quarter-hour show in her period called "Musical Kitchen," which I wrote and emceed, it was simply too much. There was no time to devote to the preparation of "Musically Yours," so one of the happiest times of my broadcasting career had to come to an end.

As the 1950s approached I noticed a definite trend at the CBC; I began to see a waning of radio commercial time on the network because of the advent of TV. And I could also see local CBC radio getting a shot in the arm with CJBC suddenly becoming the CBC's personality station making it very commercially oriented.

Perhaps I should outline something that was becoming very clear to me at the time. A recollection of my first days in radio in Western Canada reminded me that there were two key periods of prime time for radio: the noon hour and the supper hour. They were the two most potential audience periods. This was long before morning radio took over that category. And so a supper-hour program appealed to me as a strong audience attraction. This was before that time slot became known as the "going home" period, or "traffic time." During this period, although the transient audience was coming up strong, it was the lonely housewife that was the key figure. I'm sure you know the type I mean, the, "you there in the kitchen, mother, bless your little heart" type of listener (no offense, Bill Deegan) who was still considered the recipient of a strong but soft masculine appeal. And so, temporarily, I started "At Ease with Elwood Glover" which became a byword of unhurried, quiet spoken, late afternoon, early evening companionship with the music more pop than jazz, quiet rather than raucous, and with features throughout like Bob and Ray, a syndicated American comedy vignette by two of the most distinguished radio comics of all time, Walter Bowles's newscast, Dave Price's or Ed Fitkin's sportscast and, later, traffic

This is another PR *photograph but one with a good deal of truth in it. When I was doing record programs like "Musically Yours" a substantial amount of what was one's own time was spent previewing music for use on the show.*

reports from the Ontario Motor League usually delivered by graduates of the Ryerson Institute.

You'll notice I planted the word "temporary" when the "At Ease" program started because I want you to know the CBC does not believe in jumping in and committing itself to something it might regret later. Seventeen years after "At Ease" started I received from the CBC Director of Radio, Jack Craine, a memorandum which read (and I quote from memory), "We are pleased to confirm your assignment as host on the 'At Ease with Elwood Glover' program over CBL, Toronto, 4:30 – 7:00 PM. John Rae [Supervisor of Announcing Service] has suggested . . . that it is about time someone confirmed you in the assignment. Take my word for it, that's the worst thing that could happen to you. Programs that are confirmed are much more likely to be replaced or pre-empted than programs whose origins are lost in the mists of time." The memo was dated 22 March 1968 – seventeen years, one month and six days after the program started! No one ever accused the CBC of moving too precipitously; on the other hand, maybe it was just a trial period and somebody up there just couldn't make up his mind. In any case, the prediction of doom for a confirmed show was wrong by at least three years; I signed off the last "At Ease" show in February 1971, twenty full years after its beginning.

I cannot leave the fifties without the fondest recollection of a program called "Juke Box Jury." (Seems every radio station, American and Canadian, had a "Juke Box Jury" back in those days.) This was a weekly half-hour show at 7:00 PM every Saturday on CJBC devoted to the solemn judgment by three "experts" as to the merits of certain record releases and their chances for longevity, which at that time might be as long as two and one-half weeks. It used to amuse me the seriousness with which we took this sage appraisal; the weight of decision rode heavily on our shoulders. Careers could be made or broken on our decision on whether a record was a "hit" or a "miss."

The jury consisted of Dick MacDougal, Byng Whitteker and myself with Drew Crossan our producer. Each week three selections would be chosen by our producer from the hot and eager hands of local recording-company representatives and although we never gave it a passing thought these hard-working experts in public relations would race back to their superiors with the joyful news that "Juke Box Jury" was going to judge their latest hot release. If it got a hit rating there'd be joy in the streets that night and another record representative's wife would be taken out to dinner that weekend. One of the mysteries to all of us was why Mr. Crossan would occasionally choose the flip side of the potential hit for some vague unexplained reason that the chosen selection gave a better "curve" to the show's pacing despite whether we were judging hits or not. Ah, the wonders of Lorne Greene's academy! Its graduate students retained to the end what they'd been taught about the elements of good programming. I'm sure readers of *Cashbox* or *Billboard* thought we'd either missed our weekly issue of these bibles of showbusiness know-how or we'd taken leave of our reputed experts' senses and had lost all touch with current choice.

We were a world-shaking triumvirate alright. MacDougal's whimsical indulgence of a type of music he held in complete contempt gave the program balance and sanity. Whitteker with his determination that anything less than "Ellingtonian" was hogwash and me with my sense of unerring proportion, my inate awareness of public taste, my scholarly analysis which would take on the boredom of an academic treatise and put everybody to sleep as witness the audible yawns often heard from my two colleagues. And the guests we had! All the record companies would do their damnest to get their artists to visit the show – live. Even if they were appearing at the old Town Casino in Buffalo, they would be brought over to Canada especially for a guest appearance. Stars like the Four Lads, Nat Cole, Margaret Whiting, Gordon and Sheila MacRae, Sammy Davis Jr., Frankie Laine, Johnny Ray, Tommy Edwards, Joni James, Carmen MacRae, Guy Mitchell, Rosemary Clooney, Les Paul, Mary Ford and Tony Bennett. All of which made it kind of weird if a famous recording star had just turned out a dog of a record and we were inclined to pan it. There must have been something about the age then. Hosts were kind to guests; you could kid them, tease them a little, but probing dissection, investigative needling, purposely making the guest feel embarrassed – none of these things were thought of in the early 1950s.

I remember Peggy Lee sitting in one day. We were reviewing her rendition of "Lover," a Gordon Jenkins arrangement. The panel was caught up with the frantic tempo of this record, as against the languid, easy-paced rendition of the vocal. Near the end there is an animal-like wail as the arrangement begins to ease somewhat from the hysterical pace. I asked Peggy Lee what was the significance of such an abrupt change-about. She answered with straightforward candor, "That was Gordon Jenkins's interpretation of the female orgasm." Well, after audible clearing of throats and several "Well there, now thens . . ." the panel speedily went on to something more profound and less erotic.

A moment I will always cherish was after the taping of the program, Peggy Lee took me over to a corner of the studio and sang a full chorus of a new song she had worked on with her husband, Dave Barbour. She asked me what I really thought of it because she wondered why it wasn't a bigger hit than it was. Can you imagine being sung to in that intimate, breathy manner of a Peggy Lee – with her staring right into your eyes – for thirty-two whole bars and be expected to form a syllable, let alone an opinion? Maybe you remember it. It was called "I Don't Know Enough About You."

Another star we had on "Juke Box Jury" was Kay Starr. I remember being impressed with one of the flashiest smiles I'd ever seen with acres of teeth. A pair of pale blue eyes shining from a face so dark I thought she was an Indian. Turned out she is.

The jury's opinion of her record – not so good. It had a raucous background, jarring, raspy voice quality and edgy pitch. All in all, a record that was not only a miss, but a gross mistake in judgment on somebody's part. It could have set Miss Starr's career back ten years. The record was called "Wheel of Fortune."

Another up-and-coming young singer appeared as a guest during the panel's review of "Boulevard of Broken Dreams." His name was Tony Bennett. So pleasant and unassuming, never arrogant or pushy, so quiet and self-effacing that all three of us decided that he'd never get anywhere. He just wasn't hard enough to take the knocks the entertainment business could give him. I recall Byng and I offering advice to him after the session. He seemed so eager to learn. He literally asked us our candid opinion of his possibilities as a record singer based on the sound of his first attempt with Columbia records. We rubbed our respective chins (Byng's three and my two) in deep contemplation. We agreed it was a passable effort for a first try, but there did seem to be a noticeable strain on the high notes; there was a slight wavering of pitch on the low notes and, in between, the diction could be a little more polished. He nodded appreciatively and agreed that he felt it would probably hold back

the success of the record and our jury decision that it
was merely passable was a fair one. Both Whitteker and I
had a guilty twinge of conscience for being so frank. We
hated to be responsible for sending another young hopeful
down the drain to oblivion, especially when he was so quiet
and retiring and not too sure of the future.

Byng Whitteker was a strange guy. I first met Byng in
1939 when he joined the Toronto announcing staff after
having been banished to Windsor, Ontario, for some mis-
demeanor. He was senior to me by six months. He had
joined the CBC in Ottawa in the fall of 1937. When he arrived
on staff in Toronto his reputation had preceded him. He
was big, gruff, impatient with authority and a great jazz
fan. When he found out I was too, we mutually decided
what the CBC needed was a first-class jazz show. Can you
imagine a jazz show on the CBC in 1939?

The Toronto area was under the rigid, autocratic rule of
one Dick Claringbull. He dearly loved to put the fear of
God into any employee weak-kneed enough to shake in his
boots when he fixed his piercing eyes into one of his never-
blinking glares.

And yet our program actually happened. Around 1940
the CBC's secondary station, CBY, was badly in need of programming material. The CBC was to have its first jazz record-
show. Whitteker and I were given two hours – 3:00 to 5:00
PM – on Saturday. I can't quite remember how we arrived
at the title, but after jousting ideas with, I think, a suggestion from higher up that some identification with the
station should be used, it was decided that the most descrip-
tive name would be the "1010 Swing Club". The 1010
(pronounced "ten-ten") came from the frequency on the dial
which at that time was CBY's location. CBL was at 860. The
first program was a definitive discography of Louis Armstrong, one of Byng's favorite jazz artists. He picked the
records and I wrote the script.

The first feeling of tension between Byng and me was not
long in coming; after the show was over, co-hosting it as
we went along, Byng had the temerity, and I suppose,
honesty, to tell me he didn't think much of the script and
where did I get the idea that I was a jazz expert. Actually,

I wasn't. I was a dance-band fan. (See *Bands Canadians Danced To*, published by Griffin Press and available at your local bookstore.) Bands of all sorts were my passion. Some jazz I liked, some I didn't. Some I still don't. But I was eager for education in everything, having only recently come from the prairies to what I considered the Mecca of all knowledge. In any case, it was my first introduction to the Whitteker candor and in many ways a somewhat overbearing manner that, as I found out, was abrasive to others as well. Yet we managed an unspoken truce through the pioneer stages of the legendary "1010 Swing Club" through its phases as a record show and into what was a first for any CBC jazz show at that time, a live audience, "Dance Matinee." This was the "1010 Swing Club's" attempt to broadcast from a real nightclub which for some unheard of reason met with the approval of a galvanic Mr. Claringbull and the program management. The first thing we knew we were broadcasting 3:00 to 5:00 PM from the Club Top Hat with Frank Bogart and his orchestra and such vocalists as Betty Davis, Bette Morrison, and musicians like Teddy Roderman, Vern Kahanan, Jimmy Reynolds, Gordie Evans, Reef McGarvey and others to whom I apologize for having forgotten. Now I remember: Byng and I used to alternate these shows – one hour for the recorded portion at the studio, one hour live from the Club Top Hat. Two full hours of wailin' jazz from the staid old CBC every Saturday afternoon. And the guest bands that we used to feature! (How we got the budget I'll never know.) Sabby Lewis from Boston with an up-an-coming young trumpet player that stunned us all with his high register work – his name was Cat Anderson, later a stalwart with Duke Ellington. There was Red Norvo with one of the great small bands of his career that featured Specks Powell, Aaron Sachs, Shorty Rogers and Eddy Burt. There was Fats Waller and his rhythm, an engagement made more memorable because the Top Hat was one of the last engagements before his all-too-early passing.

I remember how we instituted the first celebrity interview idea with name band-leaders that came to town. The Palais Royale was the first source of these followed by the Silver

Slipper, the Masonic Temple and the Mutual Arena (now the Terrace). How they came! Almost one every week – Freddy Martin, Eddy Duchin, Jack Teagarden, Les Brown, Bob Crosby, the Casa Loma band, Bunny Berigan, Artie Shaw, Charlie Barnet, Duke Ellington, Count Basie, John Kirby, Jimmy Lunceford, Stan Kenton, Louis Prima, Charlie Spivak, Woody Herman, Glenn Miller. What collector's items those interviews would be today; they were on old, sixteen-inch aluminum discs and where they are now nobody knows. What a contrast with today: Now, if you want to interview anybody, you just sling a Nagra around your shoulder and tape the whole world. In those days we'd have to get Roly Anderson to take out the mobile unit, a huge truck used for CBC actuality broadcasts, which we'd park, usually beside a convenient window, run the mike cable into an office, jack up the sloping corners of the truck assuring a flat, horizontal surface for a smooth unwavering track for the recording turntable.

My memories of some of the people we interviewed in those days? Well, let me see. I can recall the terrible pressure that fame seemed to inflict on Glenn Miller. The moment he stepped into the dressing room at intermission at the Mutual Arena, and saw me waiting with a microphone in hand, he turned like a cornered fugitive to his manager, Don Haynes, yelling, "What the hell is this?" And Haynes, who was a placid man, assured him soothingly that it was a legitimate broadcasting station not some fly-by-night reporter trying to get to him without permission. Another perturbed musician was Eddy Duchin who took vehement exception to the small crowd that turned up at the Palais Royale and was impatient bordering on discourtesy during my attempt to interview him.

It seems that my meetings with Duchin were destined for edgy discomfort; five years previously, during the summer of 1937, while visiting my favorite dance-band locations in Chicago, I happened to be staying at the Palmer House with the specific purpose of being able to visit the Empire Room where the Duchin orchestra was playing. He was one of my favorites from my radio listening days in Western Canada when the late-night dance remote was one of my links with

Guy Lombardo, London, Ontario's gift to "the sweetest music this side of Heaven," returns to his native land for "Fitch Band Wagon" from Maple Leaf Gardens, 1943. That's E. Glover, announcer, in the background, right.

the outside world. Duchin, like Lombardo, was assailed by critics and ridiculed by legitimate pianists, but, he had flair, dashing good looks and he was there first. He was the originator of piano playing, society, band leaders. Many followed: Henry King, Nat Brandwynne, Carmen Cavallero and Joe Reichman. In many cases they were superior musicians, with greater technique, but nobody could take away from Duchin his sense of style, his ability to identify. There was no other quite like him. Duchin's presence in Chicago during my brief stay was a looked-forward-to highlight. In fact, my whole journey that summer was a result of saving my meager, hard-earned money from my first radio job in my hometown in order to tour Chicago, Toronto and New York. I wanted to see for myself all those imagined locations and radio celebrities that were so vividly planted in my mind's eye.

In Chicago it was the Drake Hotel with Clyde McCoy, Hal Kemp at the Black Hawk restaurant, Duchin at the Palmer House, the Bismark with Art Kassel, the Aragon Ballroom with Wayne King, the Trianon with Jan Garber. In Toronto it was the Royal York with Horace Lapp, the King Edward with Luigi Romanelli, Joe de Courcy at the Old Mill, Trump Davidson at the Club Esquire. In New York it was Lombardo at the Roosevelt, Emil Coleman at the Starlight Roof of the Waldorf Astoria, Jerry Blaine (I remember it well) in the non-air-conditioned rooftop ballroom of the Park Central Hotel, Blue Baron at the Edison, Nat Brandwynne at the Essex House and Sammy Kaye at the Commodore.

I'd be twenty-two at the time and the reality of sitting through the supper show, alone at a ringside table in the Empire Room, not even knowing the proper silver to use and what all the goblets were for, was an exciting dream come true. To a kid whose big moments in life, so far, involved a Saturday night at Temple Gardens in Moose Jaw, or a rare trip to the Trianon in Regina and the dance pavilion at Lake Manitou, this was quite a step forward. To me, even hearing the Silvertone Seven from CKCK or Leo Smuntan from CFQC Saskatoon was exciting enough but here I was in Chicago! With typical youthful brash I remember going back of the bandstand during intermissions to talk to members of the band who at that time included violinist Milt Shaw and trumpeter-vocalist, Lou Sherwood. When they found out I was a Canadian, they thought I'd be interested in meeting Duchin's road manager, Bill Young of Toronto. He immediately took me under his wing because of mutual friends we had back in Canada. Bill Young made me feel right at home during my brief stay. When I asked about the chances of meeting the famous man, Bill seemed to sidestep the issue for some reason, the nearest I could gather was that things were not well behind the scenes. Finally, when I did get introduced amidst a crowd of fans around the piano, it was as if I never existed. For a guy who had lived for this moment it was a traumatic let-down – the handshake was limp, Duchin talked to someone over my right shoulder without even a glance of acknowledgment. Even Bill Young seemed embarrassed by the incident. When we came back to my table, I became insistent about the situation and asked Bill bluntly to account for Duchin's aggravation. After a brief hesitation, I finally got the story which was to make headlines all over the country two days later: Marjorie Oelrichs Duchin was in serious condition in a New York hospital during expected childbirth and the news was not good. Eddy Duchin was leaving the next day for New York to be with his wife. There were thoughts of cutting the Chicago engagement short – that concerned me more than the thought of poor Duchin's personal situation. But when I read the news in the *Tribune,* I knew Eddy Duchin's seat at the piano would be unoccupied for some time to come. Milt Shaw, the violinist, carried on and fulfilled the date. Mrs. Duchin's death during childbirth was the biggest blow in her husband's life and a shock to the social and medical world at large. Friends tell me Eddy Duchin was never quite the same again. So when I recall that meeting at the Palais Royale I realized things were not the same even after five years. It's possible that Eddy's career had suffered because of the tragedy. Peter Duchin was brought up by the wealthy American diplomat Averell Harriman who was a close family friend. Eddy disbanded and joined the navy shortly after the Toronto engagement and was destined to die of leukemia at the early age of forty two in 1951.

For those who saw the movie *The Eddy Duchin Story* starring Tyrone Power, there were a lot of tangents and sidelights that did not actually happen, but the basic story is actually true. For those who remember it's interesting that Averell Harriman became a character called Sherman Wadsworth as played by Shepard Strudwick. James Whitmore played the part of Lou Sherwood who, instead of being a trumpet player, played the part of Duchin's manager.

An amusing note to remember about the old Palais Royale was the jovial co-owner, George Deller. He was an old showman from the carnival days and rose from being a weight guesser to a partnership with Bill Cuthbert of one of Canada's most famous dance palaces. He dearly loved to entertain the big names that would visit the Palais Royale and every one-nighter was open house in his office for press and celebrities alike. I remember he used to love to emcee on the bandstand occasionally and call the spot dances between sets of the Bert Niosi orchestra. To this day I can remember a favorite catch-phrase of his that I never could figure out. He'd call out, "Okay, friends, next dance is a spot dance and here comes Rusty." I must ask his daughter, Marlene Smith, a leading theatrical producer in our town, exactly what her father meant; nobody else seemed to know.

As the "1010 Swing Club" passed on to other hands, Byng Whitteker's and my association ceased until the "Juke Box Jury" days of the early fifties. Byng's career leaned more towards outside broadcasting and originating shows like "Byng's Choice" and "Small Types Club" with that familiar instrumental theme, "Teddy Bears' Picnic." How well I remember when that song was introduced 'way back in the mid-1940s by a nine-year-old called Ann Stevens, back in my old "Musically Yours" days.

Byng also liked to produce live musical shows, "mood" shows we called them, such as "Starlight Mood" starring Esther Gahn and Bruce Webb. Byng had a determined set of ideas of what constituted good broadcasting. No doubt these were Byng's happiest days. Happier even than his days as co-owner of the Celebrity Club with Jimmy Shields. This was a social club for the entertainment profession on Jarvis Street in Toronto, across from the CBC. It opened 2 April 1957. (As Jimmy Shields assured me, "We didn't dare open on the first of April – the odds were too much against us.") Jimmy has told me the whole idea of the Celebrity Club was born in the CBC coffee shop one day, when Byng Whitteker told him his ambition was to own a pub. Jimmy Shields at that time was interested in purchasing a hotel. When Byng realized that Jimmy was interested in the same thing – and had the money to do it – Byng said, "Jimmy, if you have the money, I can get the license."

Although the Celebrity Club still operates in the same vein, it now seems to be patronized by the advertising and business professions. In its heyday it was the focal point for every actor, musician, radio performer and celebrity that either resided in, or visited Toronto.

Byng loved good food, good liquor, beautiful women and rarified moments of conviviality and good conversation. He presided over the club with all the authority of a wealthy potentate. I recall he was a great admirer of Ernest Hemingway (whether this led to Byng's interest in Spain and bullfighting, I'm not sure) and when he was holding court at the Celebrity Club I often thought he sometimes seemed the embodiment of all the frustration and dreams of past accomplishment that seemed to occupy the last part of Hemingway's life. In my opinion the Celebrity Club was a solace to Byng's bitterness over the passing of radio's more halcyon period. He knew the medium was no longer his to wield his own brand of rough, yet tender magic. Whiling away the hours at the club always seemed to me his determination to live as rich and full a life as the years would allow. They didn't allow much. The radio world mourned one of its true originals when Byng Whitteker died on 27 January 1970 at the age of fifty six.

Dick MacDougal was another true original. Dick was more than a jazz disc-jockey. During all the times I heard Dick on various jazz shows – as far back as the old CKCL days – the true MacDougal personality was never allowed to overshadow the music he featured. He always seemed to keep himself in check. He loved the word "facilities" and he'd drop it into as many sentences as he could. His on-air patter was usually sparse and seldom garnished with the jazz vernacular of the time. Yet, in his off-air conversation he was as hip as the most ardent cool cat. He loved "groovy," "wild," "grand" and "crazy" but you always had the feeling that he was kidding the genre whenever he'd slip into the current jazz jargon. In person he had a most sophisticated and satirical sense of wit. He was never a great raconteur nor did he ever wax rhetorical about the aesthetics of jazz like a Nat Hentoff or a Barry Ulanov or a Robert Fulford or even a Patrick Scott. But he dearly loved it for what it was; to him jazz meant enjoyment as expressed by a true fan, the thrill and the admiration for the genius behind it all.

As an observer of the ludicrous and pompous he was masterful. His, "Hiya fella," accompanied by a rapid blinking of the eyes and the wide, close-mouthed grin and you knew you were in for some sparkling conversation or, perhaps, some devastating put-down of a blustery, super-square fellow announcer. Yet his barbs were never brutal though they could be piercing. Dick's personality was almost an act; he always seemed to be "on." You never really knew what he was thinking seriously and I often wondered if there was anything really serious that he thought about. Aside from his devotion to his wife and many children and his love of jazz, I don't think there was anything else in life for Dick MacDougal.

What television did for Dick MacDougal was like what money does for Rockefeller – he blossomed, although I assure you, not financially. He was a natural. You cannot define what it was that he had; the whole screen seemed to light up with a personality projection that no one could learn from nor could it be taught. His round, semi-quizzical, funny face just set you off before he could utter a word. The natural hipness all of a sudden was there to see, which radio could never reveal. The more ludicrous the situation that Percy Saltzman, Elaine Grand and Dick MacDougal would get themselves into, the more Dick shone as a truly magnetic star.

The whole country was stunned in February 1957 when the news spread that Dick MacDougal at the age of forty-one years was gone. I don't think I've felt a greater loss. The sobering effect it had on the entire radio and TV profession was not simply the early loss of a truly great performer and friend but the stark reality of the toll television can take. Dick lived for his new career; it was an obsession because he knew he was good, he'd found his mark. I used to see him come off shows soaking wet, perspiration dripping and clothing soaked right through. I knew the cost to his nervous system, he being overweight and fighting it unwisely plus the tension of doing too much simply sapped his strength and his heart couldn't take it. I still believe it: Television killed Dick MacDougal.

It's strange: Byng Whitteker could offend me, even infuriate me and often did. Dick MacDougal never left your company without making you feel better. Yet both were

This is a classic public-relations photograph. That's Violet on the left and my daughter Sharon, age five, apparently attempting to rouse a drowsy announcer to face another day. The clock on the bedside table – if you can see the hands – reads 6:55. The kicker? No morning-show man gets up that late! So far as I know the picture has never been published – until now.

giants of their craft, Byng Whitteker in radio, Dick Mac-Dougal on television.

Back in the forties and fifties, though, the deaths of these two originals were still a long way off. They were great days to be alive and every day dawned with the promise of new things to do, new things to say, new ways to work with this medium called radio.

One of the things about radio that fascinated me from the beginning was finding names for the programs I originated. Titling radio shows has always been fun. As far back as 1936 when the radio bug bit me and I was an embryonic announcer at my home town station, I inherited a record program from a local musician who had relinquished a jazz show on which he purported to wax analytical (he was a professional musician and knew of what he spoke). When he gave it up through boredom, I was a fledgling fresh from a bit of dance-band experience. So I decided to talk about music instead of performing it. I continued the series in the same format but I dubbed the show with the profound title "Dance Music Analyzed." Can't you imagine the comment of George Simon, the editor of *Metronome* magazine, if he ever got the word that some kid in Western Canada had decided to go on radio and tell the public how a dance band functioned and what salient points to listen for? Yet, I considered it no presumption whatsoever and I delighted in extolling the merits of the Freddy Martin tenor saxophone section or describing in minute detail how the trombonist (Russ Morgan) achieved that "moo-aw" effect with mute and bathroom plunger. The hours it took to cue the exact four bars for illustration by means of a soft wax pencil running a circle on a revolving 78 disc.

Yes, titling came easily. I simply tried to describe what was to follow with as much schmalz as possible. (There's a word – schmalz – that should place me in a proper time span.)

So, later, when I joined the CBC and through patience and diligence I was able to create my own shows, the titling becoming easy because programs that I became responsible for revolved around one thing – me. I was always a person who believed in the personality projection on a radio program; I always felt, rightly or wrongly, that a show of any nature rose or fell on the way it was presented. O, sure, the announcer was only the framework of the content, but the content would somehow just lie there if no one took the trouble to move it along or at least enhance its appeal. That is how "Musically Yours" was born.

It's a little vague how it all got started. Harry Boyle was in charge of network radio then and I remember through the 1940s I never took summer vacations. This was strange to some people on staff but I never had any trouble falling into summer fill-in programs because that was when the big network features took the summer off. I was involved in quite a bit of commercial work in those days and it, too, would take a hiatus from June to September so it left me free to step briskly into the program director's office, burning with ambition, ask what plans were afoot for, say, 1:15 to 1:45 PM daily during the summer months when Bert Pearl's

"Happy Gang" would be off the air. Maybe my audacity aroused their curiosity but I was quick to find that they were all for anybody – (anybody already on staff, that is, and therefore requiring no fee) – to fill in the summer months with a cheap little record show. Little did they know my life's ambition was to fall into what I called day time, prime time and be heard right across the Trans-Canada network in the spot reserved for Bert Pearl, whom I consider to this day to be one of the greatest variety artists Canada ever produced. So, to be a summer replacement for the "Happy Gang" program – that was arrival. What did I care about holidays? They were for people who thought radio was work. And while we're on the subject of filling in for the "greats" of the winter time periods, some years later I dreamed up a live prime time, night-time show called – (are you ready for this?) – "Glover's Lane." It featured Art Hallman, Shirley Harmer, the Bill Brady singers and Johnny Burt's fifteen-piece orchestra with Drew Crossan as producer. (How often our paths crossed.) And guess where that one was scheduled – on Thursday nights 9:30 to 10:00, a summer replacement for "Wayne and Shuster." I felt like the proverbial bridesmaid, but never you mind, it was air exposure in prime time. You couldn't buy that these days. Imagine, the hallowed time slots of the "Happy Gang" and "Wayne and Shuster" to practise what I hoped to do well at some future date. I never could understand why summer vacations seemed so important when a career was at stake.

Many aging radio listeners still ask me about "Musically Yours." It was born in the spring of 1947. Harry Boyle or someone must have been listening to the summer replacements I'd been doing because I was asked to program one half-hour of recorded music, Monday through Friday, to the East and mid-East networks from 2:30 to 3:00 PM. With the assistance of Len McColl of the continuity department we set out with an idea that would bring to fruition something that I thought was long lacking – the personal approach to a record show, classical and pop. It had yet to be attempted on a network noted for a stuffy and formal approach to matters musical. I couldn't think of anything more appropriate to call it than what it was meant to be –

"Musically Yours," a show slanted directly to the dilettante, the broad taste, every kind of music with the feeling that each listener could consider it for his or her own special pleasure. I chose the music and McColl wrote the basic outline of a script. (Len was a prince; never once did he register hurt or frustration as I would wander into a myriad of tangents or get off the track altogether.)

The show turned out to be a product of its time. The very informality and pre-disc-jockey approach must have struck a responsive chord with the listener. The reaction was phenomenal. Simply by personalizing the presentation must have been the key to its appeal. My approach was to

In 1950 I was asked to emcee a charity variety show from the stage of a theatre in London, Ontario, at 2:30 in the afternoon. The same Sunday evening I was committed to "Singing Stars of Tomorrow." There was no way to do the London show and make it back in time for a 6:30 rehearsal. No time, that is, until the RCAF offered me the use of a Harvard aircraft and a pilot. We flew to London at noon, made the 2:30 curtain, and were back in Toronto in plenty of time.

share my wide-eyed discovery of much of what I, too, was hearing for the first time. It must have brought the listener into an orbit of revelation on his own. You wouldn't believe how Litolff's "Concerto Symphonique" played by Irene Scharrer, Ann Stevens (nine years old), singing "Teddy Bears' Picnic," German soprano Erna Sack, Edith Piaf and Stan Kenton all seemed to meld into perfect company that never seemed to be even slightly unrelated. So, it was a halcyon period, 1947, 1948 and 1949 when "Musically Yours" for a brief half-hour every afternoon, seemed to be a period when people who liked phonograph records got together with somebody who was as thrilled with them as they were.

Maybe this was the beginning of what, years later, I was to be so thoroughly criticized for – my publicly expressed approval of people and things that I liked. This was a time when radio listeners delighted to share in that enthusiasm, a quality all too rare now in this cynical age when much is suspect. Today is an era when this display of approval is considered not quite the thing to do. We're all so 'hip' today that instead of relaxing and enjoying something we spend our time probing and dissecting so we'll sound erudite when we converse with our friends.

By the way, "Musically Yours" brought to me the experience of what a lot of folks thought was an undeveloped but amiable feud. I began to hear rumors of a crotchety old radio character from the Maritimes taking potshots occasionally on his country-music program. He was called Rawhide. I was suddenly dubbed with a new name; it came out something like "Ale-wood Glow-ver." To this day I've never had the nerve to ask Max Ferguson whether it was a rib or was he kidding "on the bias" (which differs slightly from "on the square").

I must tell you of a last approach to commercial network radio. It was an attempt at a Canadian-produced soap opera. I was assigned as narrator and it was for the spring and summer season of 1956. The series wasn't bad – just too late. TV had already arrived. The series was called "Brave Voyage" and was produced by the renowned CBC producer Esse W. Ljungh. It starred Corinne Conley, (who later went on to star as Phyllis Anderson in the American day-time

The beard was grown during a six-week recuperation in 1959. I wasn't able to go to the CBC so I solved the problem of broadcasting the "At Ease" program by turning my rec room into an announcer's booth. The recordings and commercials, of course, were cued in from CJBC.

program, "Days of Our Lives") George Robertson, Arch McDonald, Iris Cooper and an up-and-coming young radio actor named Larry Solway as the romantic juvenile lead. I savored those days because I knew with the end of "Brave Voyage" another era would disappear forever.

It was one day early that year I went into John Kannawin's office (he was then in charge of radio for the Toronto region) and I said, "I'd like to do something with that half-hour at 12:00 noon on CJBC, it seems to be occupied with nothing consequental. I think I could build it into something of listener interest, would you let me try?" The answer was yes and I suddenly thought of what I've already stated sometime back: The ideal broadcast periods are the noon hour and the supper hour. "At Ease" was going along well. What can I do with the lunch hour? That's it! That's what I'll call it . . . a luncheon date. "Luncheon Date with Elwood Glover."

"Luncheon Date" was a half-hour radio program from its

inception in 1956 until the fall of 1963 and continued as a simulcast for one year. In the beginning the program originated in the booth studio of CJBC and consisted of pop records, commercial spots, public service announcements and the occasional interview with celebrities from in or out of town on topics of local interest.

It was never anything else but a local show introduced by an elaborate theme called "Midnight in Monte Carlo" written by Joe Venuti and played by Joe Venuti with the Paul Whiteman orchestra which had dramatic pauses and swooping strings through which I could weave a flowery introduction. The show was unscripted. In fact, ever since the days of "Musically Yours," which was a pioneer show of its kind, I grew away from the printed word, more and more relying on anecdotes, amusing items, current headlines to intersperse throughout the program as I saw fit. This experience proved invaluable in later years because as I became more involved with daily programming, the pressure of turning out an hour or more a day, made script writing an impossibility.

Sometime in 1962 I had a telephone call from a man I hadn't seen since my earliest years with the CBC. When my wife and I first set up housekeeping in 1939, the closest drugstore was a few steps down the street and it was run by a kindly man named Koffler. His young son, Murray, worked for his dad during the summer vacation from his own studies in pharmacy. Murray Koffler was a born charmer; in his late teens and early twenties he was an affable, agreeable, thoroughly likable young man. Whether delivering a bottle of aspirins or helping behind the counter in the store, he was always a pleasure to deal with. Here, then, in 1962 was Murray Koffler calling me. After a few preliminary remarks in which we established that we both remembered the other, Murray asked, "How'd you like to do that noon-hour show of yours from the dining room of the new hotel across the street from CBC headquarters?"

Murray Koffler, druggist . . . new hotel on Jarvis Street?

Murray explained that he and two partners were building a new hotel opposite the CBC's "Kremlin." The hotel was to be called the Four Seasons Motor Hotel and would cater to a clientele that would lean heavily toward show business people. It sounded good to me and I told Murray I'd check it out with the CBC management and phone him back. Again they approved and in the fall of 1962 "Luncheon Date" moved to the Four Seasons from which it did not part – with minor exceptions – until 27 June 1975.

So "Luncheon Date" continued to develop as a radio show from the corner table of the new hotel's dining room with one operator, Herb Mais, and with records still played from the studio when music was needed. Many of my guests were temporary residents of the Four Seasons while others were brought in by public relations people. There was an excitement to the show at this time; most of the luncheon crowd paid little or no attention to me except when a well-known figure would come over and sit down opposite. Then heads would turn and murmurs would be heard above the usual buzz of conversation. This gave the program a sense of immediacy and vitality.

Then, in 1963, CBLT management (represented by John Lant and the then head of variety programming, Len Starmer) wondered if "Luncheon Date" would be adaptable for the television medium. I didn't know and said so. (Along with a multitude of reasons for doubting the possibility was the ever-fresh memory of my several denigrations at the hand of the medium.) But, I suddenly thought: This could be *my* show. I would have a hand in producing it, it would be my way of presenting a program. I'd not be harried by several people telling me what to do. The prospect of an opportunity to operate freely gave me renewed confidence. I thought, why not give it a try.

But converting a radio show to television requires more than just training a camera on a face. A camera – even a solitary camera as on "Luncheon Date" – requires mobility and to get the necessary freedom of movement in the Four Seasons' dining room would have meant removing as many as six or seven tables. It was a loss of revenue no hotel could be expected to assume. Other locations were discussed and, since we wanted to stay with the hotel which had become associated with the show, we finally settled on a lobby location. In front of a large window overlooking the entrance and driveway, a desk was installed for my guests and me, a suitable area for camera mobility was marked off and we ran a few test shows as the daily radio broadcast carried on as usual. After each test we'd all dash back across the street to a CBC screening room and view the kinescopes. The first tests were scary. Naturally it's hard to get used to yourself as an image, an identity. You see the flaws, the mannerisms. You're staggered to see what is projected to the viewer. The greatest leveler in this world, if you have a sense of self-importance, is to see yourself as others see you. The first reaction is: what an unattractive, insufferable bore you must be! Is this what your friends put up with and are afraid to tell you? Anyway, as we gained experience – on-camera as well as technical – the "kines" showed a steady improvement and, finally, on 14 October 1963 CBLT programmed "Luncheon Date" locally from noon to 12:30 PM.

The program went through several stages. First, a half-hour, then an hour. Then it went back to two half-hours with an American soap opera in between. Finally it went back to an hour with stations along the network added gradually as they requested the program. For several summer months we were expanded to ninety minutes June to October. For all that time, until 1970, the program originated from the desk by the window in the hotel lobby and was produced by three people – a producer, a public relations representative and me. How unobtrusive we must have been there in our little corner; many times during the commercial breaks people would come up and ask if I was Travellers' Aid or which way to the rest rooms.

At first, the new TV show was broadcast as a "simulcast." A simulcast was a television program that was simultaneously broadcast as a radio show. In other words, a Toronto listener could pick up the show on his TV set with the audio volume turned off, and hear the same program over his radio tuned to CJBC.

In 1970 the Four Seasons opened a discotheque downstairs and asked what I thought of the idea of moving the program to the new room complete with stage and tables set up cabaret-style and where lunch could be served. I presented the idea to CBC and once again a new phase of "Luncheon Date" occurred.

We now had a full-fledged entertainment show with a trio for the music and a small budget for talent. The name of the new room – The Studio – came about in an interesting way. Setting up the flood lights from the ceiling was an insurmountable job every day. The hotel management cooperated in allowing the lights to remain permanently. That, with the cameras standing prominently on the sidelines and photographs of the program in action lining the walls, it seemed appropriate to call the room The Studio. The name remained throughout the program's lifetime.

Whatever success the entertainment phase of the "Luncheon Date" program had was due to a most important ingredient: the musical background. Without good musicians who can play everything, who are personable and feel an involvement with the show, you can never have a closely-knit rapport. The Sonny Caulfield Trio was of enormous help in giving the show an aura of good fellowship, affability and deep concern for the product – whether in solo or group performance or while accompanying guest artists.

I don't really know how they came to join "Luncheon Date." The initial preparation for the program's guise as a variety show was handled by a dapper young man in his second production job, Nigel Napier-Andrews.

I can remember saying goodbye to Debbie Reynolds on 29 July 1970 upstairs in our lobby location. That night I was in hospital for a kidney removal with the promise from my surgeon that I'd be back on my feet, ready to start the new "Luncheon Date" on 6 September. He was right on schedule. The Caulfield trio was among the first of the show's new personnel – how delighted I was with the choice.

Drummer Bruce Farquhar, in my opinion, is the most tasteful in the business. No matter what is called for, his dynamics are always what is required, never obtrusive, but always in there providing drive and a basic beat. He's the favorite of Jackie Cain and Roy Kral when they come to Toronto. He travelled with them for five years throughout the US and Canada. He started his professional career when he was sixteen years old with the Mart Kenney Orchestra. He has toured with the Cliff McKay band and travelled through the Middle East, Cyprus, France, Germany as a member of the Bert Niosi band with a show headlined by

Tommy Hunter. He has worked with Jimmy Amaro on "This is the Law."

Farquhar's association with Sonny Caulfield began with a local CBC television show called "Sunday Morning" and later another called "Islands and Princesses."

Bruce's versatility is proven by his ability to play everywhere from the pit of the Royal Alexandra Theatre for Broadway musicals to small-group jazz at local clubs. He works constantly making records, commercial jingles and he does a considerable number of film scores with people like Ben McPeek and Jerry Toth. How lucky we were to have Bruce Farquhar on a regular basis five days a week.

I'm quite sure Jimmy Amaro is polygamous.
He loves his bass fiddle as much as his wife (that will bring instant denials from both of them). Jimmy's artistry with his bass is second to none in the country. His first instrument was the saxophone. (He comes from a musical family; his father, a saxophonist-orchestra leader and his brother Eugene, being a great tenor saxophonist.) He studied music from the age of eight and was a pupil at St. Michael's where he was a member of their famous boys choir for years. He's been playing bass since he was sixteen. His first regular TV show was a local show called "Nightcap." He is the musical director of "This is the Law," for which he composed the theme music. He has played for many theatre productions; everything from *The King and I* to Gilbert and Sullivan to Jacques Brel. He's in constant demand for the Toronto engagements of Vic Damone, Leslie Uggams and has worked for Jerry Lewis, Petula Clarke, Liza Minelli and Henry Mancini. We almost lost him once. Five years ago the Fifth Dimension (a pop singing group) asked Jimmy to join them as a permanent member of their group. However, that conflicted with his then four-week "Luncheon Date" commitment. He intended to join them when the series ended. He never got around to it – four weeks grew into five years.

What can I say about Sonny Caulfield that I haven't said publicly over and over again. He provided the ideal musical assist to the "Luncheon Date" program. Heading the excellent trio, he also sang as no other singer could to please the type of audience the program encouraged. He is essentially a night performer, at home in the dim romantic atmosphere of a cozy lounge or bar but he was able to transfer that intimacy to the vast day-time television audience. I can't ever remember reading a nasty letter about Sonny Caulfield. Both men and women viewers found him warm, sincere, retiring, but not shy. In fact everything Sonny did gave "Luncheon Date" a certain tone and dignity no other artist could have.

Sonny Caulfield was christened Allan Campbell Reid Caulfield (Sonny makes it easier). He started playing piano at the age of nine and by fifteen was playing at amateur nights and at various military bases. He spent the better part of two years in the Royal Canadian Air Force. At the age of twenty two he returned to civilian life and started a full-time career as a night-club pianist and emcee.

Sonny once auditioned as a radio announcer and was offered a staff job with an Ontario station but he couldn't afford it! The entertainment business in Toronto beckoned and in 1968 he joined CBC-TV as musical director of a series called "Sunday Morning." While still engaged with "Sunday Morning" Sonny became musical director and featured performer on "Islands and Princesses," the show that launched John Perrone, the guitarist, and Herbie Helbig, the pianist-arranger. It was Nigel Napier-Andrews, who had directed some of the "Islands and Princesses" series who invited Sonny, in September 1970, to join the "Luncheon Date" program.

With few exceptions, "Luncheon Date" remained in the Four Seasons, week in and week out. For most of the sixties and seventies, we located at the Canadian National Exhibition for three weeks – "live" every day. For one week during Expo '67 we moved to Montreal and for ten days in each year during 1971-3 we taped some seventy to eighty interviews per visit in Great Britain for use on pre-taped programs during three weeks each January to give the staff a vacation period. In 1973 we moved to Toronto's Casa Loma for a location special . . . But that's a story for a later chapter.

In the thirteen years "Luncheon Date" existed as a radio- and TV-talk show from the Four Seasons we presented thousands of celebrities to our audience and who knows

101

how many as far back as 1956. In checking back over the program's log sheets recently, I calculated we had interviewed some 11,500 celebrity guests. That's a difficult figure to perceive. Put it this way and you'll see my dilemma: Every day of "Luncheon Date" I interviewed between three and five guests, between twenty and twenty five per week. When you consider that the show was telecast fifty-two weeks of the year you'll begin to appreciate the sizeable proportions of our guest list. Sure, we interviewed many guests more than once – just as you see some friends more than others. Consider, if you will, the fact that during one of our ten-day trips to England, we came home with seventy-eight ten-minute spools of film.

I cannot make mention of "Luncheon Date's" staff without mentioning Bruce Lowry. I frequently referred to Bruce on the show as our "unofficial official photographer." For nine years, from April of 1966 until the last show, Bruce covered the program with his camera; his files include more than 3,500 negatives of show business celebrities and his photographs of "Luncheon Date" guests grace these pages.

Whenever I'm drawn into a discussion of "Luncheon Date," the question inevitably comes up: "What was the most memorable show you ever did?" My answer usually varies, depending on who asks the question and how I happen to be feeling at the particular moment. Many programs remain indelibly graven on my mind and I don't quite rightly know how I should weigh and assess the merits of each.

However, if you'll allow me to re-phrase the question: "What shows produced the greatest viewer reaction?" then I can answer with ease. There were three programs which drew more mail than I thought the post office could handle. They were Stompin' Tom Connors's wedding, an appearance by singer, Keath Barrie and the first appearance of poet Terry Rowe.

The minster who married Stompin' Tom and Lena on 2 November 1973 had written a special wedding service. By the hundreds viewers wrote asking for a copy of the service.

For those of you who haven't read it, I reproduce it here.

MINISTER: "Entreat me not to leave thee, or to return from following after thee; for whither thou goest I will go; and where thou lodgest I will lodge; thy people shall be my people, and thy God, my God."
Marriage is the oldest and most beautiful rite in the world. Love sanctifies it; understanding strengthens it; courage gives it endurance; and peace, with each other, gives it a quality of timelessness. Hope, trust, and have faith in each other, but above all these things, love one another; for love never fails.

> O grant me nothing in my soul
> May dwell, save thy pure love alone;
> O may thy love possess me whole,
> May joy, my treasure, and my crown:
> Strange fires far from my soul remove;
> May every act, word, thought, be love.

If you, Lena, and you, Tom, have taken into consideration the true meaning of your wedding vows, and you are both free and willing that this marriage now proceed, will you affirm it by the joining of your right hands.
Shall we pray:
Father, we pray for the happiness of quiet, simple things, for contentment that comes from looking at a pot of flowers on a window ledge; at the light of an open fire on the hearth, or the colors splashed across an evening's sky. We pray for the happiness of harmony in our home, of mutual cooperation and goodwill. We pray for the happiness of being, as nearly as we can, at all times, honest, and sincere, and true. We pray for the inner joy that only eternal love knows. Amen.
Do you, Tom Connors, take this woman, whose right hand you now hold, to be your wedded wife; promising to love her, honor her, and to keep her in sickness and in health, and to be her faithful and true husband?
TOM: I do.
MINISTER: Do you, Lena Walsh, take this man, whose

right hand you now hold, to be your wedded husband; promising to go where he goes, live where he lives, and through all of life's chances and changes, to be his faithful, loyal and true wife?

LENA: I do.

MINISTER: May I have the symbol of the vows that Lena and Tom have given to each other today? Thank you. Lena and Tom, will you both please look upon this ring, symbol of your wedding vows, and listen to what I say concerning it, and you.

From the elements of the earth, through work and faith, was wrested the material for this ring. Just as from the elements of life and emotion, came your desire for this marriage.

This ring was worked and refined by those who knew its value, until it has become what it is today – a beautiful symbol of triumph and unity – without beginning and without end.

You, yourselves will know the worth of your marriage, its weaknesses and its strengths. But all that marriage can be, comes only from the work and refining that you two put into your basic desire, and from the purity of that desire. Work the material of your marriage, with the knowledge of its pricelessness, and the toil will be as nothing; while the joy and beauty will last you both throughout your lives. Work together, like the fire and water worked in the purification of the gold in this ring, and your companionship will grow, your love will blossom, and your strength in one another will increase a hundredfold. Only believe in the material of your marriage and the end results, as the makers of this ring believed, and you shall succeed in the end, with a marriage of very great worth; remember

> True love gives –
> Forgives – outlives –
> And ever stands
> With open hands.
> And while it lives –
> It gives.
> For this is love's prerogative

> To give – and give – and give.
> May this golden circle, emblem of untarnished eternity,
> be the sign and the seal of a pure and unperishable love
> now mutually pledged.

TOM PLACES RING ON LENA'S FINGER

MINISTER: And now by the authority invested in me by the Province of Ontario (and by the higher authority of God), in the presence of these witnesses, I now pronounce you man and wife.
> The Lord bless and keep you;
> The Lord make His face to shine upon you
> And be gracious unto you;
> The Lord lift up His countenance upon you
> And give you peace.

TOM SALUTES HIS BRIDE

On 4 July 1974 Keath Barrie touched another emotional chord in the Canadian psyche when he quoted in full a long poem he'd written titled "On Being Canadian." Again, the mail was fantastic.

ON BEING CANADIAN

1. I met a Man the other day
   His name was Smith or Brown.
   We started talking and he said
   He lived in Toronto town.

2. We had a couple of drinks or so
   While small-talk carried on –
   The weather, car and cost of things
   The game the Leafs had won.

3. But then he got more serious;
   He spoke of wife and kids,
   Promotion he was slated for;
   His thoughts on Politics.

Keath Barrie

KEATH BARRIE
Keath Barrie comes from Alberta. He lived in Hamburg, Germany during World War II and during much privation. He returned to Calgary in 1950 but came East in the mid '50's where he worked as a prop man and set decorator, which was the closest he could get to show business. He wrote songs with no success until someone suggested he should record them himself. He did so with little or no encouragement. Somebody must have been wrong. Keath claims his appearance on Luncheon Date was the turning point of his life. He is now an important recording star with Canadian Talent Library.

4 He told me what he thought was wrong
  With how the Country's run;
  That those who want to separate
  Should all be shot or hung . . .

5 That Britain who had won the war
  Had given Law and Queen
  Tradition and a Heritage
  That call for our esteem.

6 The fellow was sincere enough
  And much he said was so;
  But when we parted – I was sad
  Just why, I didn't know.

7 But then I met another Man –
  This was in Trois Rivières.
  We had some business to discuss
  And papers to prepare.

8 Well, after business talk was done
  We shared a bottle of wine
  And talked of weather, cars and cost
  – Just like the other time.

9 Again the conversation turned
  To Kids and Home and Job,
  And Politics got in there, too,
  And how Quebec was robbed.

10 He also knew all that was wrong
   With Governmental Types;
   How it was time that *they* got *theirs*,
   The time for equal rights.

11 The French, he said, were there before;
   Why should they show esteem
   For British culture and its law
   And bow before its Queen?

12 The Fellow was sincere enough
   And much he said was so;
   But when we parted – I was sad,
   Just why, I didn't know.

13 Thereafter I met other Men
   Of diff'ring origin:
   Of German or Ukrainian
   Italian and Finn.

14 They all took pride and meant to keep
   A Culture handed down
   From ancestors long dead and gone
   Who worshipped different Crowns.

15 Each had their heroes painted red
   With blood from conquered Foes
   Saint relics of barbaric past
   And slaves who kissed their toes.

16 Oh, true, each had their Poets too,
   Their building artisans;
   The music and the painting greats,
   Those diamonds in their sands.

17 These things indeed are things to keep
   Remember and adore
   But they are not the things that cause
   For Men to go to War.

18 What matters then Napoleon
   A Henry One or Eight,
   A Frederik or a Catherine?
   Just what made Caesar great?

19 Be honest with yourself and know
   That what they won was wars.
   It was not their humanity
   That opened all their doors.

20 Then find a Man from Anywhere
   Who'll find a cause for war
   In Haydn, Bach, Sibelius,
   Michelangelo, Renoir –

21 I know now why I once was sad
   When talking to those Men;
   They're Strangers in this Land of Theirs
   They're Not Canadians.

22 And now I am no longer sad
   It's anger that I feel
   With Men who can't tell Good from Bad,
   With Men prepared to kneel

23 Before the Altar of the Past
   Sublime and out of reach
   Placed there by Men who cannot share
   And Bloody Venom Preach.

24 Don't be a Fool my Good Friend Brown
   Nor you good friend Patou
   Cause I'm Prepared to share with you
   Your values that are true.

25 And I don't give a damn about
   The Hist'ry of your Kin
   Cause you were never part of it –
   You're a Canadian;

26 But it is time you realized
   Your glorious Fate and Chance
   That lets you live in Canada –
   Not England – and not France.

Somewhere in the depths of an old CBC building in Toronto there is probably a room full of statisticians whose job it is to calculate to the tenth decimal place the number of pro and con letters each program generates. My sympathy to them for such detailed accounting but I'm glad you did.

As for me – when I counted myself a staff member of the corporation – I was always eager to know whether the mail was predominantly favorable or unfavorable. When dozens upon dozens of viewers wrote ecstatic letters praising Charlie Farquharson, my production staff and I made a point to have Don Harron on the show regularly. When thirty-five listeners objected to a tie I'd worn on a show, I made sure I didn't wear it again, not for a good long while, anyway.

Now, what does all that mean? Well, it means that I haven't the foggiest notion of how Stompin' Tom's wedding, Keath Barrie's reading and Terry Rowe's poem (patience, it's coming) stacked up in the "race" for most mail. And I don't think that standings are that important. What *is* important is that the old values – love, sacred (Stompin' Tom) and secular (Terry Rowe); and pride of country (Keath Barrie) – prompt most Canadians to write letters. Certainly these three programs were the highlights of "Luncheon Date's" history.

Terry Rowe's first "Luncheon Date" appearance was on 1 November 1972 shortly after his first book, *To You With Love,* was published. Terry, who's a very comfortable, easy guy with a face described by one writer as looking "like he's been there and back again," agreed to read from his poems. The CBC's switchboard lit up like a Christmas tree. Bookstores were sold out within an hour. Terry returned several times to the "Luncheon Date" show and each time he read more of his love poems. I conclude that there are a lot of people "out there" who are seeking to clarify for themselves the mystery, the meaning of love. That, it seems, is Terry Rowe's mission as well. Here is one of my favorites from Terry's third book, *You and I, and Love.*

Terry Rowe

TERRY ROWE
Terry Rowe – a Luncheon Date success story – one appearance with his poems snowballed "To You With Love" into over a hundred and thirty thousand copies sold in the U.S. and Canada by March '75. Not bad for a Grade 8 drop out who ran away from home at 13. Publishing the book himself after three turn downs, these warm thoughts forced him to change his unlisted phone number twice in six months.

CHANGES

I used to be that way too,
thinking it was the big,
expensive things that were important,
especially if they were new.
But lately I've learned
that a peanut butter

sandwich made with fresh
bread, and ice cold
unsalted butter,
tastes as good
as filet used to.

Sure I like riding
in a Cadillac,
but I don't care
if ever I own one.
I can sit for hours
now in a beat up pick-up
truck,
just listening to life.
Those other days when I
had to keep going,
keeping up with the Joneses
was fun,
but not enjoying life.

I used to sit for hours
in a bar insisting
on Chivas Regal,
but now I know
after the third,
a little glow,
they all taste the same,
the only real difference
the name.
Just like vin ordinaire,
after many,
no difference from the rare.

On the train or plane,
it used to be only
first class,
now,
standing in the aisle,
nose pressed to frosted
glass,

happier,
watching the countryside
rolling by;
one of the happy,
unhappy people
now am I.

I consider the last five months the most successful in the program's eleven and one-half years as a TV show. Two reasons: First, although I was exhausted long before this, I felt relaxed and free. I wasn't as uptight or emotionally distraught as I had been. The fact I knew it was coming to an end seemed to relax me. I felt I had nothing to prove anymore. Second, the choice of guests had never been better. Look at some of the names – everyone of them a star, though not all were performers – Henry Fonda, Hume Cronyn and Jessica Tandy, Anne Baxter, Frank Sinatra Jr, Warren

The "Singing Stars of Tomorrow" was as good as its name – it was the springboard for many a young Canadian opera star.

Beatty, Tony Randall, Jack Carter, Don Rickles, Gordon Lightfoot, Erica Jong, Germaine Greer, Buzz Aldrin.

Suspecting there was a desire to change the show in its 1975-6 season, I did not feel up to dealing with any up-dated changes the CBC may have wanted. I felt that December 1974 was sufficient notice to tell the CBC I desired to be relieved of the show in June 1975.

Since then – since June 1975, I mean – I've spent a lot of time thinking about my career, my life, my future. One thing I've pondered is what would I do differently if I ever got to do it over. In other words, what are my regrets.

Well, let's see . . . Maybe I should leave my regrets for later in the book but here I would express one big regret – that I never fought back like I should have against the newspaper critics, those human carrion-eaters. Read on, my friends.

Photographs by Bruce Lowry

Charlie Farquharson

Barbara Hamilton

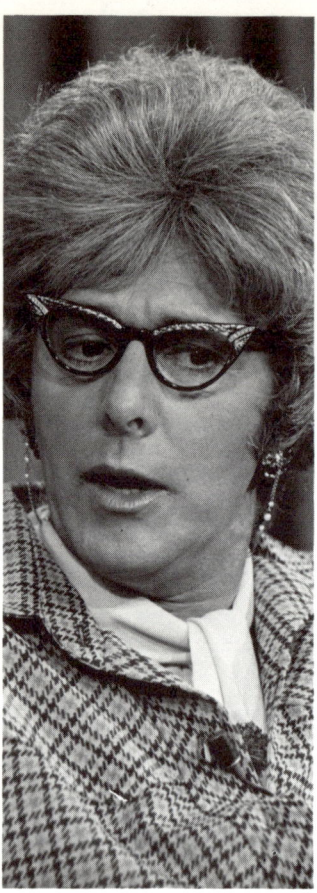
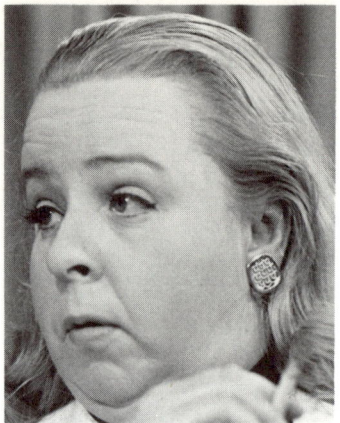

Don Harron's alter ego, Charlie Farquharson, is so complete, so compelling that I forget an actor named Harron exists. Charlie is a complete individualist and a mangler of words *par excellence*. Don Harron has been working on the creation of another character, a snooty, nose-in-the-air woman named Valerie Rosedale. When Don played Mrs. Rosedale on a "Luncheon Date" program in 1975 his performance prompted a letter from one listener who wrote: "I was pleased to see Charlie Farquharson playing the part of Mrs. Rosedale." High praise, indeed, when a comic character is so well portrayed that he completely submerges his creator. *(23 April 1975)*

Barbara Hamilton is one of Canada's most gifted comediennes but she was also a lifesaver for "Luncheon Date." On numerous occasions she was called at the last minute when another guest failed to show up. It's a measure of Barbara's intelligence and wit that she *can* fill in at a moment's notice. Throw her a line or a simple question and she would use it as a springboard to the funniest, thigh-slapping routine. Her wit is often sharp and pointed; on one occasion she ripped into an airline – Canada's own – and why we weren't sued I shall never understand. Barbara says she's a scatterbrain and leaves all kinds of messages to herself stuck to the refrigerator door with magnets. "I always see the notes – I go to the refrigerator quite often," she says. Yet she complains frequently about her weight and on one occasion I suggested to her that the location of her reminders was simply encouraging between-meal snacks. I wanted to suggest she tape the notes to the handlebars of her exercycle but I didn't want her to slug me. *(8 April 1975)*

Stanley Myron Handleman

Stanley Myron Handleman is one of the more subtle, cerebral comedians now appearing on the night-club stages. He personifies the little man, the one who is always abused by those larger than he is or by those in authority. He must be listened to – he has no highs and no lows. He jokes about himself: "I'm often on stage for several minutes before anyone laughs." But once you follow his thought processes the punchline often hits you right between the eyes. Someone once described Handleman's technique: "He delivers material through a maze of unconnected absurd situations." Right on. His humor is soft and gentle but often enough I get the feeling that under some of his stories is an element of hurt and pain. I get the impression that he took his knocks as a youngster. *(20 May 1975)*

Marty Feldman

In the movie, *Young Frankenstein,* Marty Feldman plays the hunchbacked ogre, Igor ("pronounced Eye-gore" as he explains). It's a departure for Marty because he's been a comedy writer rather than a performer. But with his ready wit and his amazing ability to pop his eyes to an alarming degree, he should go far as an actor-comedian. Somehow, the "Luncheon Date" producer discovered that Marty was an accomplished jazz musician and, on camera, presented Marty with a flugelhorn. Marty proceeded to demonstrate his expertise for most of the interview and took a solo with Sonny Caulfield's group. He's a thoughtful, articulate man who wears his newly-found fame with pride and humility. He's a warm human being. *(5 February 1975)*

Victor Borge

Victor Borge should be a compulsory interview for every aspiring talk-show host; if you can survive your first interview with this brilliant and witty man chances are you'll go far in show business. On the several occasions I interviewed him I managed to get a semblance of seriousness out of him, but not often. By and large his quirky humor pops out and tears any attempt at a straight interview to shreds. There are three questions I've learned that one never asks Borge: "How did you come to America?" ("By cattle boat," he is likely to answer.) "Is your piano just a prop for your comedy?" ("Yes, I lean on it every performance.") and "How do you find your audiences these days?" ("O, I just look out and there they are.") I think Borge hates interviews; he finds most of the questions ludicrous, monotonous and repetitious. A final question to avoid with Borge is, "If you had your druthers, where would you like to be at this moment?" Quick as a flash he'd answer, "Anywhere but here!" *(11 October 1973)*

Peter Cook   Dudley Moore

Interviewing Peter Cook and Dudley Moore is like walking on eggs – it must be done with great caution. There's no doubt they are imaginative comedic geniuses but when they exercize their talents off stage they amuse themselves with "in" jokes so obscure that they are the only ones who appreciate the humor. Dudley Moore, who is the pianist of the duo, has a disconcerting habit of mugging outrageously when Cook is being questioned. Cook makes a real attempt to answer the questions but eventually he breaks up at Moore's off-camera mugging. The interview collapses on the studio floor. One soon abandons the thought of a serious interview and simply falls into the role of straight man. Not what I would call a successful interview – but a lot of amusement nonetheless. *(25 March 1975)*

Don Rickles

I think the funniest part about the Don Rickles appearance on the "Luncheon Date" program was not on the show itself but when Don walked into the dressing room before the program. We were introduced, shook hands and sat down. Then, the strangest experience. I was testing him out and he was testing me. He'd ask me a few questions and I'd answer – a kind of investigative procedure. He was trying to find out what kind of a guy I was and I was trying to figure out how he was going to be when he came on the show. I'm a Don Rickles fan and I've watched him on other talk shows and he can go crazy-mad when he wants to. The thing about Don Rickles is that he's like a time bomb set to go off and if you give the magic word he explodes in all directions. On the air he was great. He answered my questions logically and with clarity. (Which is more than he's done on some talk shows.) I was very careful not to lead him into a situation which he could develop spontaneously and turn the show into a shambles. My key question to him was: "How do you know when to pull back? How do you know when you've gone far enough with your insults without getting people angry or without turning the audience against you?" He says it's an intuitive thing he's learned over the years. He stumbled on the idea of being an insult comic purely by accident. He was playing a cheap night club in Florida. One night the audience was unruly and insulting, so he turned his act completely around and started to insult the audience. Instead of turning on him as he expected them to do, they started to laugh. That was the beginning of Rickles's new act; he discovered it is possible to make people laugh when you insult them. He practised his routine until he could hone the insult to a fine stiletto-like point so he could get right to the heart of the victim, give him a rough going-over and still pull back before he got angry. I can assure you that Don Rickles is a very sensitive man. Everybody says Don Rickles is a pussycat at heart and he is – he's polite, thoughtful and considerate but I think underneath the Don Rickles's personality is a hurt that goes 'way back. The whole theme of his comedy is to point up the bias in man's bigoted nature – to tear down the walls that protect him from the slings and arrows of others. I believe this is an age when we're beginning to be a little embarrassed by the hypersensitivity we show towards racial disparagement. We're all people, says Don Rickles, let's stand up for the individuals we are, not the pigeon holes we're put in. That's why I think Don Rickles is the comedian of the "now" generation. *(June 1975)*

Bob Newhart

Away back in 1960, in a San Francisco night club, the hungry i, I did a radio interview with a young, new, fresh comic named Bob Newhart. Bob had catapulted to fame with his first record containing a hilarious account of a driving instructor. At that time he was being hailed as one of the most exciting new comedic finds working the night-club circuit. Bob was working as an accountant – "the world's worst" – when he started playing club dates as a comedian. When he discovered that others laughed at the same things he did, he concentrated on his act and forgot accountancy. At the time of this interview he was really quite unhappy about playing club dates – "everybody in a night club has something else on his mind – drinking, romancing a girl. The customer isn't really interested in hearing a comic routine." Bob said he preferred playing concert dates at colleges but never once mentioned TV, the medium which eventually brought him his greatest fame and fortune. *(September 1960)*

Rich Little

In the beginning which was Ottawa, Rich Little was a fine mimic but the quality of his material was still to be refined. I have the first record album he ever made, mostly impressions of Canadian politicians, and although his sound was uncannily accurate his material was not what you'd call big time. Rich and I used to kibbitz around a lot when he appeared as a guest on "Luncheon Date." He liked me to play stooge to his ad lib routines and I can see now that he was practising and perfecting his ability to extemporize, a facility that improved with repeated exposure on US talk shows. As is the case with all the best mimics, Rich manages to look like the person he's impersonating; I don't remember who he was playing when this photograph was taken but it must have been one of more than one hundred characters he does, a list which is much longer today. *(25 November 1973)*

Fred Dobbs

Along with Charlie Farquharson and Henry Morgan, Fred Dobbs made regular, twice-monthly appearances on the "Luncheon Date" program. Michael Magee's alter ego is Fred Dobbs. I've always had the feeling that Michael Magee has to explode so often or he'll go berserk! He is so outraged at the inequalities of the world, the bureaucracy, the fat-headedness, the belittling of the little man, the injustices of our society, that he created Fred Dobbs to be his spokesman. I'm quite convinced that if Michael Magee – clean cut, youthful – went on TV and spoke out the way he does as Fred Dobbs, he'd be taken off the air, in fact, it would be too outrageous to believe and the audience would not accept his fury. As an old curmudgeon with the bristly mustache, the thick, matted, white hair, the beetle eyebrows, the ridiculous unpressed suit and the frayed shirt collar, the string tie and all those idiotic pins and emblems on his lapels, this gives Mike Magee the shield. This is what he hides behind in order to vent his spleen. I've admired Fred Dobbs for a long time (like Charlie Farquharson I now think of him as the dominant one, not his creator) not just for the way he strikes out at the world but for the polished sense of showmanship he has developed. As with Charlie, I've watched this happen on "Luncheon Date." A most difficult thing in TV is to acquire the ability to organize your material so that you can build toward the end of your act and just before you're out of time you come to your big finish leaving the audience hysterical and wanting more. Both Charlie and Fred had mastered this trick just before our series came to an end. Lately through constant practice Fred Dobbs has developed into an accomplished stand-up comedian. Fred Dobbs is becoming a Canadian institution.
(11 June 1975)

4

★★★★★★★★★★★★★★★★★★★★★★★★★★★★

I WISH I COULD...

... remember where I read this: "A man who is anybody and who does anything is surely going to be criticized, vilified and misunderstood. This, however, is no proof of achievement; the final proof of *that* is being able to endure it all without resentment."

Well, easier said than done. In the light of the criticism levelled at the "Luncheon Date" program which began to take on the appearance of an onslaught in 1974, I often ponder the erosion. Was it like seeing something torn asunder after achieving a plateau of expertise? Looking back near the beginning we survived reasonably unscathed. But it's strange to try and analyze a deluge that takes on the appearance of an underground campaign planned to eat away at the underpinnings. It was as if there was an evil genius somewhere saying "this show has got to go". Or it could be that as an exercise in destruction the critics simply said they had enough and they were out to convince the public that they should feel the same.

What is it that distresses them so? The fact that a TV program with such an unorthdox beginning should have gotten off the ground in the first place? The fact that Canadian TV variety programs, notorious for their low batting averages, should allow one to get out of hand and gradually build a substantial following of long-lasting fans and because it was originated and headlined by a single individual? Ahhh, that may be the rub. Canadian critics can't seem to stand an individual acquiring celebrity status due to the devotion and loyalty of a certain segment of the public. It challenges their power to destroy.

The critics are fiercely competitive. Compare the writing styles and you can see the bristling phrases sticking out so readers will go around the next day saying, "Hey, did you read what so-and-so said about such-and-such yesterday?" This is how their reputations are made. The quotes are legion. After all, it is the printed medium. Don't think for one minute that every one of them isn't writing for posterity. Ever since the line, "She ran the gamut from A to B," to "It should not be reviewed but posted like a poisonous waterhole", every critic from the big-city dailies to upstarts on small, local papers are praying for that deathless line that will make them live forever.

I wish I could remember the contributor of the most memorable quote I've ever read about critics and their function. No, it's not the one that goes, "A critic is somebody who would tell Don Juan how to make love." It was this one: "Opinions are more often the product of cynical manipulators than genuinely informed intelligence".

I often think back to 1937 when the CBC allowed an accident similar to "Luncheon Date" to happen. A last-minute frantic solution to filling in a few weeks of summer programming was turned over to a staff studio musician. "Get yourself some musicians and see what you can do", said the station manager. That was the birth of "Bert Pearl and his Happy Gang". How would they have survived the sting of criticism that would have been hurled their way? It is quite likely it would have planted the seed of cancellation immediately and Bert Pearl would never have been allowed to become the institution he was in the golden age of radio. Bert Pearl was lucky to be a product of his time. I was lucky in 1963 when the television version of "Luncheon Date" began. The first reaction was nothing. In fact I suggested that no press releases, no advance build-up be allowed until we got underway, letting the program build on its own. I recall so many of the big prime-time shows of the early sixties given tremendous advance publicity, drawing much attention to their debuts but few of them could live up to the inflated reputation they were given before they earned one of their own. And so "Luncheon Date" started slow and being scheduled up in the middle of the day, it wasn't really worth much comment from the press. The critics were more interested in the big-budget, nighttime productions. Come to think of it, day-time television back then was yet to be considered in important program planning. So for years we escaped notice. There did occur the odd laudatory word; I can remember when Bill Drylie and Roy Shields were tolerant and aware of what we were trying to do. I always privately thanked Nathan Cohen for his discreet silence at all times. I had a sneaking suspicion that Nathan respected me for the years of service I had given the industry and, because of that, he simply refrained from any critical comment. The same protection came from Patrick Scott; I used to cringe in fear if Pat Scott ever decided to do a review, but he too chose silence.

I wonder if my natural reluctance to talk to critics could have something to do with the treatment received? I once said to Bob Blackburn of the Toronto Sun that I always felt uncomfortable in the presence of critics through fear, I guess, of saying something that would give them food for comment. In the presence of critics I seem to have a conscious awareness that perhaps they expect you to be scintilating or at least humorous, so that you might come off with something so clever that they couldn't resist quoting your off-the-cuff remarks for the next day's column. (How often I wished I could be that original with *bon mots*.)

I must say however, that Bob Blackburn, though he constantly needled me, it was done with good nature and most of the pinpricks he gave me I secretly agreed with and they usually served to be constructive.

As for the other critics, I couldn't say that the relationships have been good. Oddly enough, one of the most irritating "critics" isn't even one; he's an entertainment and part-time gossip columnist who periodically takes delight in allowing bristling personal prejudices to shine glowingly. I'm pretty sure I know the reason for his malice. It's a long-standing grudge that he has kept because he feels he was ill-treated as a guest on the program years ago; I remember the circumstances very well. It was when the program was a one-camera affair from the lobby of the Four Seasons Hotel and it was during a particularly harrowing period of technical failures when, on a moment's notice, we had to run across the street, usually with five minutes to go, and breathlessly sit down in a hastily assembled studio or booth, proceed with an hour of spontaneous communication expecting the harried guests to hide the fact that they were being put through a horrible ordeal too. And I have every sympathy for guests who are uprooted, rushed and hustled about in a most tension-packed, nerve-racking atmosphere. This was one of those days. A famous American comedian was the other guest and because of the confusion and the makeshift emergency of the situation I can only assume that this reporter-columnist thought he's been short-changed and not given equal time and therefore thought he'd been made to appear in a bad light as a guest. Certainly the comedian tended to take the spotlight, but what comedian doesn't? Surely, if you've seen American talk shows, no guest who appears with a comic is ever demeaned or belittled simply because the comic dominates the situation. Anyway so much for the apparent treading on toes. By the way – there was not one word of feedback that such a slight had taken place, but it serves to illustrate what can turn out to be a long-standing vindictiveness by a member of the press. I come to the conclusion that it's very easy to fall out of favour with the press. I remember a case during my radio days with the "At Ease" program that a certain local columnist took a lengthy delight in running down the program every chance he could get. I could never figure it out; I had never met the man as far as I could remember. I had already been doing the program for several years without comment and suddenly a veritable barrage. I discovered later that he came from my hometown and although unknown to me there, who is to know what incident, what snub perhaps, might have happened back in my youth that could have upset this person.

    I think the most terrifying hunch I ever had of what the critics could do to the "Luncheon Date" program was when it was proposed to broadcast live the Stompin' Tom Connors' wedding. I was in such fear, that in the initial stages of the planning, I strongly recommended that we cancel the whole idea. The reasons were twofold: one, I never liked to allow an idea to make the program a sitting duck; and secondly I didn't want anything to hurt Stompin' Tom Connors whose down-to-earth sincerity and interest were without question.

    They were all there – every last one of them on that momentous day. When I went out to begin the show I could not only feel their presence, I could feel their hot breath as they gripped their pencils with white-knuckled determination. Well, most of you know what happened: not a word of derision. The simplicity of the occasion, the tone, the dignity, the obvious lack of any intended hoopla turned them into instant lambs and Tom Connors' second greatest moment in his life was when he uttered his moving comment following my question, "Tom, why did you do this on television?" There were a lot of strained throat muscles in the room and some obviously damp eyes. I had a feeling that the critics sneaked away quietly, sheathing their dagger-like pens murmuring, "Curses! Foiled again."

    I guess the Jack Miller and Blaik Kirby columns upset me the most. They were occasions when I decided there was definite unfairness and there comes a time when you have to strike back.

    I always knew that if you battle columnists you never

win, but there is one weapon a performer can use and
I strongly recommend that more performers use it; take
advantage of the letters-to-the-editor column – never
retaliate to the columnist personally, it only goes into the
wastebasket. But letters-to-the-editor departments love these.
You can almost be assured they'll get printed because
newspapers love controversy. I responded to the Jack Miller
column in this way because I thought he treated me unfairly.
I think it unethical to deliberately demean the career of
one person while attempting to enhance that of another.
In other words, to degrade in order to uplift is not the
highest form of journalism, and I said so. As for the Kirby
column, I decided to answer him on the air. I discovered
something that I think I knew all along – critics can dish
it out but they're not too thrilled about taking it.

Professional critics although personally hurtful really
concern me from a more serious standpoint. Readers in
general can agree or disagree or merely be amused but there
is one category of readers that disturbs me – they are the
program planners. People who listen to the critics and are
influenced by them are the ones in whose hands the fate
of a program lies. You would think the public would be
the final arbiters as to the success of a program but con-
ference room, executive-suite mandarins take it upon
themselves to accept the blame if a program receives a bad
review. That is where the critic takes on a dangerous
importance; he may pretend he's not a molder of public
taste and he isn't, but he certainly can manipulate top-
mangement sensitivity. A critic's scathing review usually
has a message and management thinks it's trying to tell it
something. That "something" is usually to improve what's
already going well or to fester an idea where the only cure is
"doctoring" or out-and-out cancellation. In all fairness I'm
making that a generalized statement because at no time
in the lifetime of "Luncheon Date" did any uneasy
suggestion come down from management. But I have to
remember that I was on staff, I always kept a low profile
and didn't make waves; as long as there wasn't too much
critical talk about the show nobody said anything. But
who is to know what went through their minds during the

critics field day throughout the program's eleventh year?
I believe the fate of many programs popular with the public hangs on the decision of the policy makers.

Canadian TV is unlike the United States in many ways. One is that the rating race alone decides the fate of American productions; CBC shows are not ruled by that system. I feel that program planners look upon critics as the super intelligentsia of the medium and that if enough of them reach the same conclusion the word gets around, "let's call a meeting".

Photographs by Bruce Lowry

Elizabeth McQuaig

Early every year the Toronto Symphony Orchestra raises money with a "dream auction" in which the public is asked to bid for some dream – a trip for two to the Caribbean, the chance to travel with the Maple Leafs, a guided tour through Toronto's sewers, a whole string of things. Mrs. Elizabeth McQuaig bid for, and won a chance to emcee the "Luncheon Date" program. Mrs. McQuaig, whose husband had recently passed away, brought her own guest and the two women discussed the problems of facing life without their mates. It was a splendid, inspiring interview. I've since lost track of Mrs. McQuaig but if she reads this I want to thank her for one of the most memorable "Luncheon Date" interviews. She was a determined lady who wanted to try what she'd always wanted to do. She carried it off with warmth and sincerity and the audience loved it. (Incidentally, Mrs. McQuaig contributed $350 to the Symphony for the chance to emcee the show.) *(27 February 1975)*

Buzz Aldrin

It's a little unnerving to interview a man who has walked on the moon. Buzz Aldrin is one of a handful who have. However, it wasn't his experiences in space that interested me so much as his experiences after he returned. The cruel and harsh glare that is the lot of the celebrity almost obliterated Aldrin, the man. Aldrin explained that his life in the military had prepared him to give and receive orders; "everything in my life led up to the voyage to the moon," he said. Within hours of his splashdown he felt the first wave of depression, an empty feeling of little left to accomplish. That was just the start. Within days of his return he found his regimented patterns of thinking blasted apart. He was lionized, idolized, popularized; his value system was eroded and destroyed. His marriage almost collapsed but Aldrin is a man of remarkable will. He came back from the brink, resigned his commission, established himself in business and re-assembled his life. A genuine hero, more for the conquest of himself than his conquest of space. *(15 May 1975)*

Robert Campeau

Robert Campeau is not in show business but he is a star. He's a one-man industry and on the air following the opening of his palatial new hotel I called him the "Michael Todd of Canada." He has the compelling magnetism and the shining aura of success that always signals the big time. Campeau began his career by building a house – one house. Now he heads up a conglomerate that, among other things, owns the glistening new Harbour Castle Hotel on Toronto's waterfront. Mind you, I wouldn't want to work for him; I have the feeling he churns up employees like a giant mixmaster. But for those who can and do work for him, it must be an exciting and fulfilling occupation. *(7 April 1975)*

Louise Tandy Murch

A few days before Easter, 1965, I heard of an elderly lady named Louise Tandy Murch who was just about to celebrate her ninetieth birthday. I thought she would be an inspiration to many of "Luncheon Date" fans who were, by and large, of mature years themselves. After that first appearance Mrs. Murch had a standing invitation to return to "Luncheon Date" on the program day nearest her birthday. In 1975 she returned and allowed us to help celebrate her one-hundredth birthday. She lives in the same house she moved into as a bride; she cooks her own meals, practises yoga, plays piano and sings. She still has a few students studying voice. She would be a remarkable woman at half her present age. She lives by three phrases: Be active; be interested; be interesting. "For heaven's sake," she advises, "get up and do something. Stir up whatever gift is within you." Her favorite hobby is playing for sing-songs in homes for senior citizens. May she live forever – a grand, grand woman.
(28 March 1975)

Roloff Beny

I'd been warned about Roloff Beny's temperamental nature so I treated him with caution the first time around. We circled like two wary dogs after the same bone. But subsequent interviews became much more comfortable. His very life style is intimidating. Poised, sophisticated, living in Rome and being a part of the European jet set makes him rather foreign to the way of life we're used to and he's all the more an enigma because his background was like any other Western Canadian boy having spent his boyhood in Medicine Hat and Lethbridge. His books are indeed the Cadillacs and Lincolns of the publishing world. An artist and photographer, his real craft is in packaging. He can turn out a book in which he is the creator literally, from cover to cover – design, choice of paper, binding, supervision of lithography, he makes the total book a work of art regardless of content. His books are glorious examples of what we have come to know as coffee-table books. It wouldn't surprise me if the name was coined as a result of Roloff Beny's craftsmanship. *(30 November 1973)*

Rolf Harris

Rolf Harris came to Canada from his native Australia and first made a stir in musical circles by performing some of the rhythms and sounds of his country's native music. But Rolf isn't a singer only; he has an amazingly wide range of accomplishments. On the "Luncheon Date" program he set out to paint a landscape using a four-inch wide house painter's brush and accomplished the task in just six minutes. It was – like his singing and clowning and sound effects – damned good. That's one of Rolf Harris's big problems; he's so good at everything he does you wind up marvelling at him more than laughing. *(23 May 1975)*

Georgie Jessel

I wonder where Georgie Jessel would be today if fate hadn't dealt him a wild card in the twenties. Jessel was offered the movie role to re-create his Broadway success in *The Jazz Singer,* the first talking picture ever made. Quarreling with the studio bosses lost him the job and the role went to Al Jolson, a young singer who sounded not unlike Jessel. Jolson, as everyone knows, built a lifelong career in the movies on the basis of that first film. Jessel, who played a few parts in movies, never approached Jolson's popularity and I suspect that Georgie is still a little hurt by it. However, he's made another kind of mark for himself as the world's most famous after-dinner speaker. He basks in the glory reflected by those celebrities he praises; he is a past master at name dropping and is one of those entertainers of the old school who will need an audience until the day he dies. I'm sure Georgie's great disappointment will be that he won't be able to deliver his own eulogy! Come to think of it, he could always put it on tape. *(19 February 1975)*

Germaine Greer

Tolerance seems more evident in Germaine Greer than when I first met her. She also seems less militant and when I suggested this she replied, "I'd like to be more militant but I don't know who to punch." She was very low key about 1975 being declared Women's Year. "We're not ready for it – maybe by 1980." I asked Miss Greer what was the primary message that the women's movement wanted to put across. "There is no simple message," she explained. "What we're looking for is the real texture of the female experience and so far it has always gone through a sort of male filter. There has always been a mask we put on; there have always been things we didn't say." I suggested to Miss Greer that what appeared to be antagonism toward men in the early days of the feminist movement seems to have dissipated. "Most feminists think that our biggest problem is that we love men. And that because of the ludicrous situation that we're placed in politically and economically, we're forced to love them in a way which is beneath us, an ignoble way. We need them as much as we love them. We must cut down on the element of need and build up the element of genuine tenderness and tolerance." A lively, thoughtful, intelligent woman. *(30 May 1975)*

True Davidson

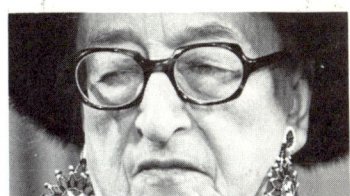

When she was the mayor of East York, a borough in Metropolitan Toronto, True Davidson was renowned for two things: her hats and her wit. For her "Luncheon Date" interview Miss Davidson wore one of her more subdued hats but didn't suppress her tongue; as you can see she looks like she's getting ready to give me a blast. In fact, we talked of politics, secrets of success, even religion. Finally, Miss Davidson said to me: "Now let's be funny ... can't we get off on something light and amusing ... like women's lib." "You think that's amusing?" I asked somewhat surprised. "Yes, I think it's pretty funny ... Most women don't *want* to be recognized as the equals of men, they don't *want* to be heads of departments in stores, they don't want to run businesses. They'd like men to want them to – but that's a different thing ..." Miss Davidson is no longer active in Toronto politics although she is now a newspaper columnist. She is one of the great ladies I have met. This "Luncheon Date" appearance coincided with Miss Davidson's seventieth birthday and I wished wholeheartedly for "many happy returns." *(19 April 1971)*

Malcolm Muggeridge

A "vendor of words" is Malcolm Muggeridge's description of himself, a deplorably brief description of a multi-talented man. His days as a caustic commentator on man's foibles seem to be in the background now; he has renewed his faith in Christianity and his deeply religious feelings are his favorite topic. He spoke of his feelings at length on the interview but here, I'd like to confine his comments to some of his views on television. "In some ways I both hate and fear television. It can be potentially dangerous but of course it is equally the case that it's impact is terrific . . . People think the camera shows reality but, in fact, the camera shows an image of reality and that image can be more deceptive and can be used more effectively for deception purposes than the most deceitful writing or talking . . . Blake wrote, 'they ever must believe a lie/who see with, not through the eye.' Now, you see *through* the eye when you look out on the world from yourself within. You see *with* the eye when your eye merely reflects the images in front of it. The camera is an instrument for seeing with, not through . . ." *(19 April 1971)*

Bob Hope

Bob Hope is an incurable showman – he *needs* an audience. I'm sure there are moments in Hope's life when he paces back and forth in boredom because he's alone, without an audience, without the sound of laughter. Laughter is like breathing to Bob Hope; he must have it to sustain life. But he's also an admitted sentimentalist. He told about crying at his youngest daughter's wedding. As he drove with his daughter to the church he had been aware of her nervousness and her reluctance to leave home. "It made me sad," he recollected, "but I didn't cry. Then we got into the church and started down the aisle. I could feel her shaking a little but I was still in control. When we reached the altar I turned to take my seat and she grabbed me and gave me a big kiss and said, 'Goodbye, daddy,' and *that* did it, that started the falls." Bob also commented on the growth he noticed in Toronto: "You're going to have a great town here if you ever get it finished." *(21 August 1969)*

Merle Shain

"Merle Shain is a soft puppy." I don't know what made me say that but it suddenly occurred to me that she's just that lovable and fragile. Merle Shain is the only magazine writer who has ever written an article about me that I thought was well done and close to the truth. Of course Merle Shain is the *only* magazine writer who has ever written an article on me. I've always shied away from such folksy stories for publication and I don't know why. Maybe because I like the privacy, I don't like revealing intimate details for public scrutiny and also because I've never thought my background, unexciting as it is, to be of any interest to anyone. (Also, I've turned them down for the hatchet jobs they usually are.) Even this book is a chore I haven't taken too much delight in simply because I can't manage to find anything about myself that is fan-grabbing news. However, Merle managed to do an excellent job of projecting what I am and made it interesting enough that at times I thought I was reading about someone else. Merle Shain to me is the consummate journalist. She does exhaustive research; she studies her subject. (She followed me around for weeks which was not at all unpleasant. We got along exceedingly well.) Since publication of her own book, *Some Men Are More Perfect Than Others,* she's a much-in-demand talk-show guest both here and in the US. She has perfected the technique to such a point that she has raised the level of being interesting on television to a highly professional degree. She has great poise; she has great beauty and enough femininity that she appeals to both men and women at the same time revealing a sharp wit, a brilliant mind and a marvellous insight into the human condition. Merle Shain has always shown me that beauty and brains are an unbeatable combination and to my male chauvinist mind that's still an all-too-rare quality in this day of the liberated woman. *(29 May 1975)*

Lillian Gish

In my opinion Lillian Gish is the "first lady" of the screen. Her career began on the stage – at which she proved herself a magnetic young actress – and went on to silent movies and made her greatest successes with D. W. Griffith. Then, when talking pictures came in, she returned to the stage playing Chekhov. Her appearance on my program was occasioned by her being brought to Toronto's York University for a special showing of her films. My most stimulating conversation took place when I was asked to drive her back to her hotel following the reception. Let me hasten to say it was the shortest drive over the longest distance! How scintillating Miss Gish is when she is animated by fond recollection. I asked her about her role as Mimi in the 1926 version of *La Bohème*. That's right – a silent opera! But Miss Gish was interested in it because of its tragic story line, which after all was a novel long before it was an opera by Puccini. What fascinated me was the power Lillian Gish had. MGM promised her everything if she would only come with them – her own writers, set designers, wardrobe department, choice of scripts,

choice of directors, and complete charge of casting. She had just seen John Gilbert in *The Big Parade*. He was to be her leading man. In fact, she was so impressed with that picture she asked for and got, the director and the entire cast – King Vidor, Gilbert, Renée Adorée, Karl Dane, Roy D'Arcy and Edward Everett Horton. Then she told me of the headaches of managing her own pictures – the battling with the costume designers, the haggling with the set people – the method of rehearsals, (she preferred the Griffith style of full rehearsal right through). Then there was the problem of both the director and leading man falling in love with her. She told me about going to a hospital to observe patients with tuberculosis in its terminal stages (for the death scene). How she nearly got killed during the scene where she grabbed a chain on a cart which dragged her along the cobblestone street. It was fabulous talking to this great lady, so informally, so privately, with no audience listening in and nobody to interrupt. I was shattered when the trip was over and I ushered her into her hotel. Great moments with great people. I think those were the rewards I earned from being associated with "Luncheon Date" for so long. How lucky I am to be able to remember nearly every precious moment. My drive with Lillian Gish for less than half an hour will be remembered a lifetime.
(22 November 1973)

Paul Anka

Paul Anka looks as if he was costumed to play the part of a Mexican bandit. In one sense the analogy fits: Paul moved in on the "Luncheon Date" show and stole it right from under our noses. His appearance was a virtuoso performance of ad lib, spontaneous entertainment, a combination of rec room intimacy with night club professionalism. He took over the program for its whole hour and never once did it fall flat. I've tried to analyze what prompted Paul to extend himself like this. I think it had something to do with the initial difficulty Paul had being accepted in his home town of Ottawa and in Canada generally. In the late fifties when he was a stripling of fifteen years, he was viewed as a pushy, egocentric kid. That image stayed on even after Paul began to make it big in the US. Canada's attitude hurt Paul, I know. But in recent years, Canadian audiences have mellowed and Paul's now accepted as a superstar in his native country. I think Paul's one-man blockbuster on "Luncheon Date" was his way of saying "thank you" to Canadian audiences who have made it fun for him to return. (I think there may have been a touch of a personal "thank you" as well; in Paul's very early days I occasionally played a few of his promo records.)
(3 November 1972)

137

Sammy Cahn

Sammy Cahn, the American song-writer appeared on "Luncheon Date" one day and it was one of the most delightful, warm and exciting "happenings" we ever had. Sammy is the perfect show-business extrovert – his voice isn't great but Sammy loves to sit at the piano and play for hours as long as someone is listening. On the day of Sammy's appearance we didn't tell him that Jules Stein, an old songwriting buddy, was also in the studio. When Sammy looked up from the piano and saw his old pal, it was a fantastic reunion, a once-in-a-lifetime moment. The two of them played a generous sampling of just about every song they'd ever written. Sammy, of course, wrote "Day by Day," "Let it Snow," and "It's Been a Long, Long Time." Sammy and Jules played their co-authored hits – "Time After Time," and the Academy-Award winner, "Three Coins in the Fountain." Sammy told me that his first big song – big in his estimation at the time – carried the catchy title "Like Niagara Falls I'm Falling for You." He had to admit it didn't do too well (which isn't too easy for Sammy to admit). Another one of his early songs carried this heartbreaking title, "Every Time You Make Ends Meet, Somebody Moves the Ends." As a dedication to the "Luncheon Date" staff he wrote four stanzas to his recent hit, "A Touch of Class," from the movie of the same name. If you can think of the tune, here's an example of his specially written lyric to a program he seemed to thoroughly enjoy.

Sandy Johnson is a research whiz,
She has a touch of class.
Carol Jamieson helps to get things done,
Now, there's a touch of class.
I must musically yield to Sonny Caulfield
To him I raise my glass;
All concerned with this show, I've learned
Have a touch of class.

(25 March 1974)

Howie Meeker

Howie Meeker is a volatile man. On his "Luncheon Date" interview I don't know what came over him but he got excited at some questions and his voice rose to such a pitch he sounded like he often does on "Hockey Night in Canada." Howie Meeker is a dedicated man and his message to young Canada is heated and direct. He believes that hockey should not be taught to youngsters until they've learned to skate, pass and stickhandle. Not until the basic movements are as natural to the boy as breathing should be get further training in hockey. He deplores the present system which forces the average sixteen-year-old boy out of the game; "the boy with a desire to play but with just average ability hasn't got a chance," Meeker says. "There isn't even a team for him. He's discarded by parents and communities alike who think the kid brothers coming up have more talent. The basic hockey skills should be taught only from ages eight to twelve. *Then,* and only then, will these pupils become eligible and ready to really learn the game." As Howie Meeker says on his TV hockey school promotion spot, "If I can make something out of him the systems got to be right." You tell 'em, Howie. *(4 September 1974)*

Arthur Godfrey

I discovered Arthur Godfrey in the fifties when he did a morning radio program over WCBS in New York. He had come from Washington where he was a disc jockey and he was rapidly becoming the toast of American radio. Arthur possessed one of the best radio voices that ever graced the air waves. As a commercial announcer, he was unsurpassed. It was this ability that made him such a great success. I interviewed Arthur Godfrey for "Luncheon Date" when he was in Toronto at the Royal Winter Fair demonstrating dressage, the art of precision horseback riding, with his horse, Goldy. Part of Godfrey's immense popularity was the man's versatility: He rode, he flew his own plane, he played a ukelele, he sang, he owned his own farm in Virginia, he was part owner of a hotel in Miami Beach, he was a TV star. He was the absolute boss of every undertaking he tackled. He was the idol of middle America; it lived vicariously through all of Arthur's achievements. People admired the "poor boy makes good" image he projected. Then, suddenly, middle America wasn't watching or listening anymore. It was a sobering lesson to me of how ephemeral public taste is and how changing values can alter the public's approbation. We must instinctively know when the audience outgrows us. Still, he was King Arthur for a long, long time. [*1968?*]

Bobby Baun

To me, many hockey players lose their interest for me when they step off the ice; an exception is Bobby Baun, the former defenseman with the Toronto Maple Leafs, is a man of many facets. He's a cattle farmer, a connoiseur of good French wines, an avid reader of serious books, a knowledgeable theatre goer, a gourmet cook. He has taken one three-week *Cordon Bleu* cooking course, learning the secrets of sole Normandie, pepper steak flambée and light soufflé. He still wishes he could find the time to go direct to Paris for the school's full course on the fundamentals of French cuisine. O, yes. He's an antiques collector, as well. I was surprised to find Bobby Baun such an erudite human being. And, while we were on camera in front of the "Luncheon Date" audience, Bob recounted what, to him was his greatest moment in hockey. It was playoff time in 1964; the Leafs and the Detroit Red Wings were going into their sixth Stanley Cup game. Baun sustained a painful leg injury but stayed in the game and scored the winning goal in overtime. Next night, on home ice, he was back as his team's spark plug and it was only after the final whistle had blown that Baun's injury was diagnosed as a broken leg! As he approaches a coaching career, he has strong feelings about today's players. "In our day we gave everything

we had to the game. Today's players do not. Today they make demands."
(11 November 1971)

Buddy Rogers

I met Charles "Buddy" Rogers on three separate occasions. The last time was when he appeared in Toronto to dedicate a plaque at the Hospital for Sick Children; the plaque marks the spot where his wife Mary Pickford's original home once stood. Buddy Rogers is mainly occupied with looking after the Pickford estate but he was, in the days of my youth, a popular movie actor bridging the silent and talkie era. "America's boy friend" as he was known. I think I saw the picture, *Wings,* six or seven times, not only for the flight scenes but to enjoy Richard Arlen, Clara Bow and Buddy Rogers, three of the biggest stars in Hollywood at that time. One of the greatest joys in my association with "Luncheon Date" throughout the years has been meeting the stars of my younger years. I got the biggest kick out of meeting all celebrities on my own ground, to talk with them and find out what they are like as human beings. I've been lucky in that I have never lost the magical wonder of it all. *(28 May 1973)*

Monty Hall

Monty Hall is the expatriate Canadian who is the host and part owner of the ABC program, "Let's Make a Deal." When he appeared on "Luncheon Date" with me we talked about the flak he has had to absorb about his TV show. The critics have hammered at Hall for years claiming his program is based on the exploitation of greed. But in spite of criticism the show continues to be one of the most popular day-time programs on American TV. My own thought is that Hall's program is a fun show; the fact that some contestants win prizes adds dimension but even when one loses, no one goes away mad. In fact, it always struck me as a party game with door prizes (expensive ones, mind you). Monty Hall resents the snide references that are made about the avariciousness of his show but he is hurt more by what he considers the lack of appreciation he experienced when he was starting out in his own country. He was certainly never given the chance for popular acceptance in Canada such as he achieved in the US. But probably the timing was wrong; Monty had considerable success here in radio but television was in its earliest, groping stages when Monty was developing as a performer. He had to go to the US to try out his talent.
(17 January 1974)

Bert Pearl

Without doubt Bert Pearl was the most creative variety artist this country ever produced. His "Happy Gang" show was a landmark in Canadian broadcasting and it was to organize a re-creation of the old show that Bert was in town. In 1975 the Canadian National Exhibition was to stage a nostalgia day for senior citizens. Bert was in town to round up as many former cast members as he could find. Bert's former image – the flashing-eyed grin, the youthful exuberance – was often at odds with the real Bert Pearl. In the days when "Happy Gang" programs were at the pinnacle of success, Bert was an unhappy and often agonized man. He was plagued and tortured by details, bureaucracy and constant frustration from always seeking perfection. I'm sure Bert simply bowed out of the show in 1955 because the show could no longer contribute to his fulfillment. He left the program in the hands of Eddie Allen and moved to the US where he has lived and worked ever since. It could be that Bert's alienation with Canada was partly his own doing. In the years that have passed since he departed Bert has had opportunities to return but for some reason they never materialized. Consciously or unconsciously, a stumbling block would occur. I think the fear of failure haunted Bert Pearl and we in Canada were the losers because of it. We lost a great showman.
(13 June 1975)

Rudy Vallee

I found Rudy Vallee a sad, bitter man which depresses me. Back in the late twenties and early thirties he was an idol of mine and a giant of his time. He was the Rudolph Valentino of radio, a man of vast popularity. His style of singing gave a new word to the language – "crooning." Later, Rudy Vallee was the Ed Sullivan of his day; he had for years "The Fleischmann Hour." It was one of the best variety programs on radio and started off the careers of such budding stars as Kate Smith, Edgar Bergen and Joe Penner. His "Stein Song" and "Whiffenpoof Song" were the million-record sellers of their day. Yet with all his success, Rudy today is a vindictive, angry man – he feels the modern bargainers of talent don't see his potential. He sees the success of TV talk shows – which he'd dearly love to do – and I think he would give up just about everything if he were given the chance to be another Merv Griffin, say, or Johnny Carson. Privately, off camera, Rudy assured me that he had telephoned, written letters, sent telegrams asking for a chance to emcee one or another talk show. His offers have been ignored and he holds this to be a terrible insult to his show business background and his personal integrity. It's a sad commentary on this superstar of his time that his conversation is a put-down of the past and a derision of today's show business scene. His language is very salty when he gets on this subject – I couldn't print it here. Yes, I'm sad for Rudy Vallee; he should be enjoying his later years, relaxed in the knowledge that he was one of the greats of his day. Rudy's appearance on the program coincided with his visit to Toronto in a night-club act at the Royal York Hotel. It depressed me to have to endure what I considered one of the bluest acts ever presented there. I guess my dismay at Rudy's current image didn't show itself too obviously; we became good friends and I still get a Christmas card from Rudy and Ellie, usually a card which features some reference to their favorite hobby, tennis. By the way, Bobby Riggs and Rudy Vallee seem to be pretty good pals. I'd love to hear what they talk about! *(25 January 1972)*

Otto Preminger

Otto Preminger is probably the most controversial movie director in the business today. I've always looked forward to interviewing him because he displays such interesting opinions and is a witty conversationalist. I think he likes being on television, likes it personally and for the publicity it gives his movies. He's a ham at heart being a former actor. The man has always been a ground breaker. Until Preminger made *The Moon Is Blue* the word "virgin" had never been used on the screen; *The Man with the Golden Arm* showed the use of drugs as it had not been shown before. He loves to play coy; with a deprecating shrug he says, "O, I don't stir up trouble." But the twinkle in his eye gives him away. He has an ingratiating habit of saying to you on the air: "How would you like to be in my next picture, I have just the part for you." It sounds so sincere but after hearing it on several other talk shows you know it's a remark never to be taken seriously. On TV Preminger is a soft, teddy bear but on the set of a movie he's a frightening despot. I watched him on location in San Francisco directing a picture called *Skidoo*. I have never felt so uneasy as when he launched into a tirade against a young actress who couldn't seem to get across what he wanted. Then, like a chameleon, he'll invite the whole cast to lunch and be at the peak of amiability. I remember on one occassion Preminger brought a young man with him who was introduced as Preminger's assistant, Erik Kirkland. I met him again on the set of *Skidoo*. It wasn't until many months later the headlines revealed that Erik Kirkland was Otto Preminger's son by Gypsy Rose Lee. It's interesting to note that barely a ripple of scandal was caused by the revelation. How different from the Hollywood of decades ago.
(7 June 1972)

Henry Morgan

Henry Morgan took a little getting used to. I think the first time I saw Henry Morgan was in 1950 when he did a late-night radio show from a restaurant in midtown Manhattan. He would sit on a small stage with a microphone and he'd talk about anything. He kibbitzed with the audience and usually culminating in a violent argument which would end when Henry would leap to his feet, gather up his notes and stalk off stage. It was a frightening sight to see Henry's temper rise and an entire audience wilt with his piercing barbs. So, when Henry Morgan came to live in Canada, I was prepared for the worst. I thought if he agreed to appear on "Luncheon Date" he would find something either boring, fatuous or maddening and stamp off in a towering rage. But, he never did. I think the secret is in knowing how to treat him. It would be pointless to try to upstage Henry, or try to outsmart him; his wit is razor-sharp and fast and no talk-show host could survive a Henry Morgan blast once he started. You feed him a few lines and hope he'll react and be carried along by the subject matter. Eventually Henry and I got along so well he became a regular guest for the last couple of years, appearing twice monthly on the program. He was a marvellous guest. He pinpricked all the little foibles, clichés and personality quirks that people revealed to him. He had an incredible knowledge of things Canadian and knew far more about our country than we did. Morgan's best line, in my opinion, occurred during one conversation when we were talking about nationalism in Canada. Morgan said: "Everybody in Toronto asks me if I don't feel guilty about taking work away from a Canadian – but nobody can tell me who he is." Henry Morgan was good for Canada; he was an astute observer of our habit-forming ways and in his columns and on "Luncheon Date" he left you with a greater knowledge of yourself and of Canada while being amusing at the same time. No matter how devastating Henry Morgan became I've never known of one viewer who ever resented him. (Various occasions, *1973*)

Norman Jewison

I think possibly the most gratifying award Norman Jewison ever received was the staging of a Norman Jewison Film Festival in Toronto in June 1975. Norm is another expatriate Canadian whose ties to this country are strong. His latest film, *Rollerball*, is causing a lot of controversy but my own opinion is that it will survive as a social comment on the mores of today's society. It is a look into the future that reveals some very possible truths. As I mention in this book, Norman Jewison was the first television director I ever worked with. He remains the same basic person as he was in the early fifties. He retains strong family ties with Canada. He and his wife Dixie and their family vacation in Muskoka, Ontario, as frequently as possible. I've watched him work with actors on a set and his quiet, boyish persuasion works wonders with the most hardened, sophisticated performers such as Carl Reiner, Steve McQueen, Melina Mercouri, Brian Keith and Hume Cronyn. He gets what he wants by simply talking to them, by being completely simplistic in his explanations and guidance. No Otto Preminger he. His list of hit movies is long but some you'll remember are *Gaily, Gaily, Jesus Christ Superstar, The Russians Are Coming! Fiddler on the Roof* and *Rollerball*. *(26 June 1975)*

Harold Town

There is no more colorful character in Canada than Harold Town. Whether in his buffalo-hide coat and his Australian bushman's hat or when he sits down beside you and sets his sights on a few ivory towers. Two of my favorite books are by Harold Town: One is titled *Albert Franck, Keeper of the Lanes* which is a labor of love by Town paying tribute to the late painter whose canvasses depicted life in the humble homes of the big city. The second book is *Silent Stars, Sound Stars, Film Stars,* a nostalgic flight of fancy illustrating Harold's love of the movie-star era with appropriate sketches of the famous accompanying the narrative. On television Harold Town is a remarkable guest. On one show he talked about a Canadian-made toothpaste that is great for the gums. It sounded like a commercial but in Town's hands it was a subject of lyrical beauty. On another show he rhapsodized about the beauty of older women. On still another he thought there should be a world language created as a "sign language" which would be much easier than learning a foreign language. He loves to knock things – Bell Telephone, Ontario Hydro, fluoridation, art curators who write books, the Canadian National Exhibition. (He once said the CNE grandstand looked like it was built by two kids with left-over pieces of a Meccano set.) And what he says about the Sports Hall of Fame and the Dufferin gate is unprintable. Harold Town is never dull and he loves to make waves! With the discovery that he can write as brilliantly and wittily as he talks he is now a sort of Canadian Voltaire flogging away at the crassness of the bureaucratic society. He is not known as the *enfant terrible* of Canadian art for nothing. He has a rapier-like invective and can turn an explosive phrase with the best of them. One of the most antagonistic sparring matches I ever read was the great feud between Harold Town and Paul Duval over some harsh words Harold wrote about Duval's book, *Four Decades*. Reading the thrusts and parries of these two hot-headed artists was a delight. Harold Town is one of the last of the great Galahads. He's the François Villon of his time. I can see him in another age as a gallant musketeer matching blades with the cardinal's guard. *(A constant guest since 1971)*

Paul Rimstead

What can I say about Paul Rimstead that I didn't say the day we both got hit with a pie in the face. That show became the most spectacular we ever did – unintentionally. Now for the truth. I had heard previously from the production staff that the intention was that Paul Rimstead was to be paid a "visit" by a "hit" man. Although I secretly resent such childish peccadilloes, I dismissed the idea at the time because I had more important things to think about but the morning of the show I phoned my producer and asked, "Do you really want to go through with this?" I kept thinking of the audience who are mostly mature people and wouldn't be too thrilled with such an exhibition but I could tell the staff had planned the big event and I felt like a straight-laced old fogey if I dampened the idea. Jack Budgell was fair, though. He said if you don't want to go through with it we'll call it off. I said no, let's go ahead and see what happens. If you saw the program you already know. Two "hit" men were engaged and although I was unaware I was supposed to be a victim, Paul was unaware that someone had pulled a double-cross. The show was a shambles. Both of us were dumbfounded because we were victims of the unexpected.

Paul claimed he'd been tipped off about the attack on him. So he meant to turn the tables and make me the victim. Something slipped up and his contract had not been cancelled. So there we were – two stunned victims of our own chicanery. I had to leave the show during station break because there was no way I could continue with other guests in such a state of disarray. I asked Sonny Caulfield to take over and certainly with no misgivings because I knew Sonny is enough of a showman that he could carry it off and also Lynn Gordon was my next guest and she's such a pro she could fill any emergency. I remember coming back after a temporary "clean-up" and Sonny was doing so well I went over to the piano waiting for the play-off cue and who should join me on drums but Paul Rimstead! All in all, a chaotic occasion. Idiocy – sure. But it made the papers. Funny thing: It made the front page of the *Sun,* the paper Paul works for and Peter Worthington, the editor, remains mum to this day. *(24 April 1975)*

Bruce Marsh

For the first time in reflecting on all the guests I've had on "Luncheon Date" I feel myself becoming inarticulate. There are no words to put on paper that can express the loss of Bruce Marsh to the broadcasting industry. He does not fit into the guest category (although he was a guest several times). He was the host on many occasions. During periods when I was in hospital or on vacation, Bruce Marsh was the first choice as a replacement. He had the driest wit, the voice of an orator and the smooth technique of a seasoned professional broadcaster. He loved to trade insults with his fellow announcers and the ones he insulted most were the ones he liked best. He loved to *thunder* his voice in group conversation and there was no doubt who was holding court when you heard that "echo-chamber" resonance roll down the corridors. During pauses he'd soberly wait for a place to jump in, his dark piercing eyes darting from side to side – checking to see that everyone was paying attention. His death was so traumatic to all around him, no one could express adequately their personal feelings. The terrible drama of the wait for a heart transplant. His unfailing sense of humor about his condition. As he said in a letter back to the staff on the 27th of January 1974 from the hospital in California, "After all this correspondence with OHIP, there arrived a form letter from them wanting to know my OHIP number! But the final funny bit is this: As God is my witness, the form was signed by a person named Gravesande. I wrote OHIP and asked Gravesande to transfer my file to another clerk. I'm not the least bit superstitious but I thought that was a little much." He once said while addressing a Rotary Club, "Most people say to me that I don't look like someone who has had four heart attacks. But then, I don't know what someone who has had four heart attacks looks like." I will never forget as long as I live, the night of March second: Helen Hutchinson and I were co-hosts of the TV broadcast during the awards dinner of the Association of Canadian Television and Radio Artists. Helen was at the entrance of the Hyatt Regency Hotel and I was at the railing of the upper balcony. As the celebrities filed in I saw Bruce and Elizabeth come through the door in elegant evening dress. I choked with emotion as I watched them surrounded by friends and fans greeting each other, shaking hands, trading quips as if it were just another night out on the town. I sensed I was seeing them out socially for the last time. Sixteen days later Bruce Marsh was dead at the age of forty eight. The Reverend Dr. A. Leonard Griffith at the funeral service in Deer Park United Church on March twenty second, 1974, said in part: "Perhaps God did answer our prayers for Bruce and is answering them now on a higher level than our human minds can understand. Is it not possible that our prayers gave Bruce to us for a year longer than we might have had him? A year that distilled the experiences of a lifetime, a year that will always be precious in our memory?"

Gordon Sinclair

Ma Murray

Putting Ma Murray and Gordon Sinclair on the same program would have to end in a free-for-all. Matching two of the most opinionated curmudgeons of our country couldn't possibly be anything less than chaos – Gordon Sinclair, the stormy petrel of radio, TV and journalism; Ma Murry the editor of one of Canada's smallest weeklies, the *Bridge River-Lillooet News*. I have to admit that Gordon Sinclair, for once in his life, had to take a back seat because nobody can out-talk or out-reason Ma Murray! I asked her about her paper, what kind of paper is it and how often is it published? I remember her answer to this day: "I'm the editor of the dinkiest newspaper in British Columbia. The place I live is so isolated you gotta scrape the bottom of the barrel. My God, there isn't a week I don't have slivers in my fingers scrapin' up the news." She talked about where she was born – Windy Ridge, Kansas – how she met her husband who brought her to British Columbia, how they started the little newspaper together. Then she told Gordon Sinclair she thought the press of the country had let the people down. "The press isn't on it's toes," she said. Sinclair retorted, "Why the press has never been stronger. The press in Canada is vigorous and healthy. We've got three newspapers in this town and all are thriving." (This was in 1970.) Then for some reason, Ma Murray got off on a raving tirade about the Columbia River Treaty. (What that had to do with the state of the press, I have no idea.) She stormed: "When the treaty came up, who did they turn it over to but a good lawyer who didn't know a damn thing about irrigation, rivers or waterfalls." Sinclair argued: "But water renews itself everytime it snows. Why didn't we just sell the water to the United States?" Ma Murray shouted: "Why if you give an American an inch, he'll take a yard. He'll even come up and grab the source of it. He'll even take the mountain the snow falls on." Throughout all this Gordon was trying to get a word in as to why she thought the Canadian newspapers were letting the people down. Ma was not to be swerved. "The Columbia Treaty was never properly ratified. Even the Americans knew they were getting too much to live up to." Sinclair interrupted: "But What's that got to do with the newspapers. . ." Obviously I saw this was getting nowhere. I changed the subject: "Why have you never gone to the big city, Mrs. Murray?" Sheepishly, she answered, "O well, I'm just a small time girl. I was born out there with them gophers and cackleberries and I just never outgrew it." Then Gordon Sinclair asked if she'd ever been sued. "Several times. I've been sued so often I got used to it." "Did you ever lose?" asked Gordon. "O three or four times. Lots of times we lived on classified ads for a whole week." As you can see a confrontation between these two wasn't getting anywhere. They were just having fun bouncing off each other. Gordon Sinclair didn't have a chance and he didn't want one. He's like everyone else in the company of Ma Murray. You're so amused, so taken in by the wit and audacity of the woman there's no point in trying to compete. Gordon knew enough not to.
(16 March 1970)

Jerry Lewis

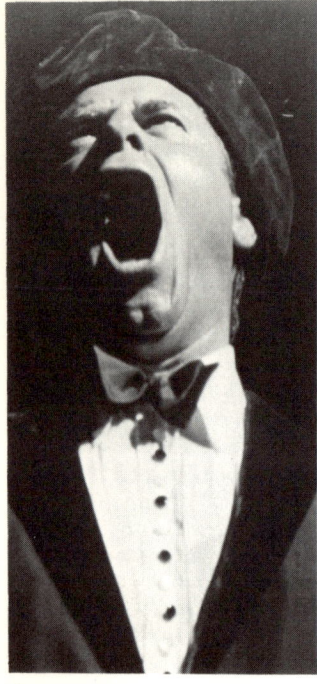

"I see things every day that appall and frighten me. The country is polluted, nobody wants to work any more, everybody is trying to do something to somebody else. We've forgotten there's an awful lot of fun in being a Boy Scout – just opening a door for a lady can be pleasant. We have an overstuffed society yet five million children go to bed hungry. The whole system is topsy turvy and inconsistent." That's a quote from Jerry Lewis made on 7 July 1966. "Who is the real Jerry Lewis," I asked him on "Luncheon Date – "the actor, the producer, the director?" "I think the director," he said with barely a hestitation. "It's truly the greatest form of satisfaction in that you're interpolating one kind of experience into another." "How does Jerry Lewis, the director, control Jerry Lewis, the actor?" I asked. "Jerry Lewis, the actor, is just like any other actor and you have to treat him with what he's begging for, care and concern. Actors are a little petulant, a little neurotic – what more can you say of actors but that they're a little neurotic?" I asked Jerry where he found the patience to be a director, worrying about a million complications; his own volatile nature, it seemed to me, would be opposed to the director's concentration on detail. "I don't know where I find the patience," he said, "unless it is underneath my whole character – a deep underlying regard for what film is. The film that we shoot today is for *ever*. I think forever is entitled to a little time. When I'm in *front* of a camera I have no time for all the technical nonsense; when I'm *behind* the camera, the technical aspects are *all* I think about and the actors had just better shut up an wait until I'm ready to project them on the public." I asked Jerry how his kids survive the notoriety of being a star's children. "Quite easily," he said, "In the first place none of my kids have ever had chums who were impressed by the children's parents. Maybe we're lucky but no one has ever said, 'Hey, you're dad's that crazy Jerry Lewis.' My kids are accepted on their own as individuals." I asked Jerry how he had reconciled his personal life with the image of Jerry Lewis. "My wife did that," he answered, "She has a very important proclamation which goes, 'Jerry Lewis is not allowed in this house.' And any time I drag him in, he's not welcome. It's taught me a lot about myself. As a director I can appreciate Jerry Lewis, the actor, when he's funny I laugh, when he's not, I cut him out. I'm luckier than most – I don't have to sit through some of his tedious humor. The kids will bug my wife, 'Hey, can we see a Jerry Lewis movie on TV? They refer to Jerry Lewis like they do, say, Red Skelton." I asked Jerry what his greatest impatience was. "That everybody makes some sense," he said. "We're not here for a long time and we should learn to appreciate life while we can. Man's inhumanity to man has got to stop. That's my impatience." *(7 July 1966)*

5

★★★★★★★★★★★★★★★★★★★★★★★★★★★★★★

THE MORNING OF 31 MAY 1973....

... 1973, a Thursday, dawned sunny and cool. As I rolled from bed about eight o'clock the sun was already climbing and a steady breeze rustled the trees. It was about sixty-four degrees in those pre-Celsius days. Perfect weather. Especially perfect for "Luncheon Date" because on this day we were broadcasting one of our occasional "location" programs, this time from the grounds of Casa Loma in Toronto. Casa Loma is a wierd and wonderful ersatz castle built in 1911 at fabulous cost by an eccentric millionaire named Sir Henry Pellatt; if the castle can be said to be of any one architectural style more than another it is probably Gothic. So it was, in the shadow of these "Gothic" walls, that "Luncheon Date" was scheduled to originate.

The program for the day was to be a modern re-staging of an "Olde Englyshe" luncheon, a medieval meal featuring dishes of the period served by buxom wenches and with a wandering minstrel in costume playing the lute. The whole bit. The program had been arranged by the British travel people to show how it's now possible to tour the British Isles visiting ancient castles, eating off the tableware with the cutlery of the times. The tours go a long way to recreate the Merrie England of the Plantagenet and Stuart monarchs. It was a colorful program, light and gay, and the hosts had invited more than 200 guests from the press and travel business to share the event. The "Luncheon Date" program had been arranged to provide the travel people with national network publicity.

That morning as I shaved, showered and dressed I became aware of something happening to my right ear. At first it seemed that the ear was plugged; I tried jumping on one leg like a swimmer trying to bounce water from his ears. Then, as more time passed, it became perfectly obvious that my hearing was going. I discussed the miserable business with Violet and we both agreed it was probably some momentary phenomenon that would disappear as quickly and mysteriously as it had come. At 10:30 I drove to Casa Loma. When I stopped the car and climbed out I was made aware, sickeningly, that the deafness had increased and worsened but, in addition, I was now strangely unbalanced; I felt as if another step might pitch me full length on the ground.

I sought out Drew Crossan, my producer, and in a voice vibrating with panic said, "I can't do the show. I'm totally deaf in one ear and I'm so unsteady on my feet that I'm afraid to walk for fear I fall down." He was sympathetic and calm. "Take it easy," he advised with cautious optimism. "You'll be okay. Sit down and take it easy. By the time we go on camera you'll be rested and your sense of balance will probably be back, anyway."

He was too hopeful. At the stroke of noon the camera's red light winked on; the program, powered by a portable generator, was being fed to the network via the CBC's studio. My guts churned in fear; eveytime I shifted in my chair I felt that I might fall. Even seated perfectly still I felt like I was toppling forward. But the dictum of "the show must go on" is strong in many of us and I managed to muddle through thirty-four minutes of the show without keeling over. The interview guests of the day had been placed to my left, in range of my functioning ear making it possible to hear their comments above the drone of the crowd.

But thirty-four minutes into the show, the portable generator, used to supply power to carry the program's signal, broke down. The studio had to find something to fill the remaining fifty-six minutes. I didn't say anything about my hearing-balance problem but I apologized to the guests for the breakdown, thanked the British hosts and rushed to my car to drive to my doctor's office, fifteen minutes from Casa Loma.

The doctor examined me and confessed to some bafflement but he reassured me that he thought the deafness was temporary and that my hearing would be back to normal within two or three days. The time passed with no improvement and I called my doctor again. When he heard of the continued deafness he put in a call immediately for a specialist and within a couple of hours I was subjected to a battery of hearing tests. The results were inconclusive. Interpreted by the specialist, the results seemed to indicate that either a virus or a tiny blood clot had hampered the flow of blood to the ear's hearing mechanism causing the nerve to malfunction and disturb my balance. The verdict was depressing: The hearing in my right ear was permanently gone.

Time passed and with it passed most of whatever degree of objectivity I had maintained until now. I was depressed and devastated; if there is one thing a TV interviewer needs in addition to his appearance and his voice it's the ability to hear what is said. My career seemed ended, my future black.

The first indication of bad news is always worse than the actual event. As days, and then weeks went by I was given a glimmer of hope by the two specialists who examined me. They agreed the hearing was totally, irrevocably gone, but they did indicate that some of the hearing might be sharpened by means of a hearing aid feeding sound to my good ear. They showed me the kind of apparatus they had in mind and it was incredibly small. I went through a number of additional, mind-spinning tests in the audio lab at St. Michael's Hospital. A wax mold of my left ear was made from which a clear plastic plug was constructed that lies inobtrusively in my good ear. Attached to the plug by a length of clear plastic tubing is a small, flesh-colored receiver that lies behind the good ear and is curved to fit. The receiver is equipped with a tiny on-off switch and with a volume control. A second curved ear lug fits behind my deaf ear and contains a microphone no larger than the head of a pin. Sound coming from the right side is picked up and carried via a fine wire no thicker than a thread to the left ear's receiver. In use, the wire lies concealed beneath the hair on the back of my head. A miniature battery, no bigger

This photograph was taken on 1 June 1973 one day after I'd lost the hearing in my right ear. I'm turned to my left to catch the words of a young woman who was my guest that day.

around than the end of a pencil, powers the unit. The whole apparatus is a marvel of electronics and miniaturization.

If I knew more about the transmission of sound I could discourse knowingly about how the hearing aid works. All I know – and for me, that's sufficient – is that this tiny miracle restores the sense of right-ear hearing. No longer am I in the truly limiting situation of hearing from one side only. The device allowed me to hear Sonny Caulfield when he talked to me from his piano at the far side of the "Luncheon Date" stage. It means that when people greet me from my right side I can hear and respond, not ignore them as I tended to do when I couldn't hear from that area. My balance is permanently gone although I discover that the balance mechanism in my left ear is compensating to some degree.

It is strange how a physical defect such as a loss of hearing and balance can alter the impression others receive. I've been told that some persons who have known me only since my hearing loss consider me to be aloof and distant. I *do* tend to ignore small talk when I'm not wearing my hearing aid but the truth is I don't hear it in the first place.

These two handicaps – the deafness and loss of balance – caused me great anguish regarding the "Luncheon Date" program. Since that fateful day in 1973 the program was a terror to me for awhile. Would I miss a guest's comment, misunderstand a word or a phrase? Would I make a misstep when I walked to the stage at the beginning of each show? So persistent was this fear that every day until the program went off the air I would go back to the CBC building from the hotel and check the videotape of the program as it was fed to Vancouver for airing at noon, coast time. I was assailed by fear that I may have missed something, may have responded to a misunderstood statement. The videotapes showed me that some of my performances were good, some not so good, but in no instance could I find a serious gaffe or blunder. O, of course, there were many times when I missed an aside or didn't fully hear the tag line of a joke. But I managed to fake successfully and the audience was never aware.

The hearing impairment sharply diminished my pleasure in doing "Luncheon Date." In December of 1974 I asked the network to be relieved of the responsibility of the program; my reasons were many and varied but foremost among them was a fear that I might let the show down. A missed cue, a question ignored, an awkward moment – I just couldn't permit these things to happen. The pressure created by my handicap often turned "Luncheon Date" into a harrowing experience. It was no longer fun. It became a dreadful chore, landmined with opportunities for error.

Even more frightening, perhaps, was re-adapting to radio.

Happy? You bet. Back in radio and glad to be there. This is the first day on the staff of CKEY, *Toronto.*

A radio announcer – a *good* announcer – learns to modulate his voice by hearing his own words, as he speaks them, played back in his headphones. Until I was fitted with electrical assistance it was a spooky experience to hear my own voice coming back from the left side only.

Life has either been very good to me or I have been extremely lucky – which amounts to the same thing. After thirty-seven years with the CBC I have retired – from the corporation but not from the profession I love. For my retirement years I plan to stay active, doing what I've always liked best, what is less harrowing, less chaotic, less exciting, perhaps, than a daily live TV show. I am back in radio, that intimate, person-to-person medium that television can imitate but never equal. My association with CKEY in Toronto has proven to be the perfect retirement plan. Not that I plan to coast on past performance; far from it. But it's good to be working again at what I've always enjoyed.

At the Cannes Film Festival in May 1973 I interviewed actor George Segal at poolside. Beard and mustache, second version.

Photographs by Bruce Lowry

Bob Farnon

Bob Farnon was the trumpet player with Bert Pearl's "Happy Gang" show back in the thirties and early forties. His work with the Canadian Army Show during World War II introduced him to England and the English recording field from which he has never returned. He remained there where he carved a considerable niche for himself as a composer of serious music and movie scores. On a rare visit to his native Canada he told me, "my musical heart is still in Canada because a lot of my music is written about and influenced by Canada. There is still a very warm spot in my heart for the country that gave me my start and especially for my dear teacher, Louis Wiseman, who first taught me my basics in arranging." A few days before he appeared with me Bob had received from England an offer (which he had accepted) to write the score of a Bob Hope-Bing Crosby film, *The Road to Hong Kong*. I remember Bob Farnon very warmly from the old days – the "Happy Gang" days, of course, and also because he was the jazz trumpeter with the three-man trumpet section of the Percy Faith orchestra in the first network program I was ever assigned to, "Music by Faith." *(14 June 1961)*

Artie Shaw

Artie Shaw is one of the most articulate men I have ever met. Shaw is amazing in his philosophy, his realistic view of life. He is truly a fulfilled man. I asked him what happens when a musician retires. "That's a difficult one to answer," he said. "Actually, I didn't retire; I became inactive as a band leader and public figure – I never did care much for that aspect of my life, anyway. I liked the music – that was a challenge – but the business of getting up and being a 'celebrity' entailed doing a number of things I never cared for. I didn't set out to do that. So it's a kind of relief to roll up my sleeves and get into another kind of work where I don't have the public watching constantly; I like to be my own critic." I asked Artie to comment on his former reputation as an iconoclast. "Well, I don't think I was ever an iconoclast," he said. "I never really set out to break anything. Rather, I'd go in one direction as long as I found myself being challenged. Then I'd branch out in another direction and maybe some people got the idea that I was trying to shatter prototypes. Life is a very complex affair; if you stay in one area for a long time you miss out on an awful lot." (Including matrimony?) We got to discussing a performer's output, whether it was "commercial" or not. "The word 'commercial' has no meaning," Artie said. "You do a thing and if people like it they buy it. Then it's commercial . . . You have to make a very broad distinction: The entertainer says, 'Here's what the audience wants and I'm going to see how well I can give it to them.' The artist says, 'Here's what *I* want – I hope they like it.' I've always tried to stay in the second category. I'm interested in what *I* want to do." Many of the big-time band leaders fell by the wayside through personal problems or early death, yet here is Shaw, one of the most temperamental, unpredictable band leaders of his era, outliving and outlasting them all simply because he refused to let the music business drag him down to oblivion. Proof that the inquiring mind stimulates the rich, full life. *(May 1961)*

Vic Franklyn

In the fall of 1972 Vic Franklyn came to Canada from Wales (Why does Wales always produce baritones, not tenors?) and he hasn't stopped yet. Vic was born "a spit away from Pontypred where Tom Jones was born" and worked as a plasterer's helper, a window dresser and a professional bodybuilder. Not all at once. His stage name honors Vic Damone and Frank Sinatra and with that kind of inspiration in his corner, the man should go far. I consider Vic to be one of the best up-and-coming entertainers now working in Canada. *(30 September 1975)*

Frankie Laine

Isn't it ironic when a singer's commercial jingle becomes as well known as his million-dollar recordings. For instance, today when I think of Frankie Laine, I can't help thinking of the line – "How do you handle a hungry man? Man . . . handlers" – before I think of "Mule Train" or "Cry of the Wild Goose." I first met Frankie when his career was at its peak in 1951. Unlike a lot of celebrities, Frankie Laine is a true and generous friend even though we've met only professionally. He loves to sit around after a show and talk – business talk, professional chatter. I remember in 1953 when I was going to Europe for the first time and mentioned to Frankie I was going to Florence. He immediately gave me the name of a friend and insisted I look him up. I did and struck up a beautiful friendship with a lovely family who played host and guide during my entire stay in that beautiful renaissance city. I've always appreciated Frankie Laine for his friendly, warm, outgoing nature. *(17 June 1974)*

Cleo Laine

There is no doubt in predicting that the name Cleo Laine will become a household word before long. Although she is jazz oriented, so are Lena Horne and Ella Fitzgerald but because of their constant development they outlived the term 'jazz' and now run the entire gamut of popular appeal. Cleo Laine's husband, John Dankworth, is a fine saxophonist, a modernist. I'm sure he was a follower of the Lee Konitz-Paul Desmond school back in his period as the leader of a big band in the fifties. Later, the film scores he wrote for such pictures as *Darling, Morgan, Saturday Night and Sunday Morning*, and others, show his masterful touch as a interpreter of modern film scoring. A friend of mine in London, named Ken Pitt, introduced Cleo Laine to Johnny Dankworth when Pitt took her to an audition at the 51 Club off Charing Cross Road in 1952. Johnny liked her and took her on a trial basis for seven pounds a week. They have remained together professionally and domestically ever since. I renewed acquaintance with Cleo in the fall of 1972 when she was playing the part of Julie in *Showboat* at the Adelphi Theatre on the Strand in London. Since then, her appearances in the US and Canada have left modern music fans breathless. She was in Toronto, at the time she appeared on "Luncheon Date," for a small concert at Convocation Hall, University of Toronto which was only partly filled. Since then and especially since her appearance at this 1975 Stratford Festival, 2 predict she will jam every concert hall in the country. 1975 is bound to be Cleo Laine's year. *(24 October 1974)*

159

Tony Bennett

Elsewhere in this book I've written about Tony Bennett – how he, as a young recording artist, was given the benefit of my advice and Byng Whitteker's, how we thought "Boulevard of Broken Dreams" was a so-so recording. Our words of wisdom to this self-effacing younger man were to get tough, harden himself for the cutthroat milieu of the recording industry. It's often difficult to admit that one's been wrong but it's an error I gladly confess to. Tony Bennett has not changed; he is still an eagerly open individual, never forcing himself on you, always waiting for what *you* want to say to him. He never lost that wide-eyed, almost naïve approach to personal relationships. He's polite, humble and truly interested in everything around him, and carries his super-stardom with grace and humility. I'm glad to count Tony Bennett a friend of long standing and if anyone wants to negate the man's singing ability, don't do it in front of me. I already did it in front of him twenty-five years ago to my everlasting embarrassment. *(14 June 1973)*

Liberace

It was away back in the early days of "Luncheon Date" when I did the show from the Four Seasons' lobby that Liberace was a guest. He reminded me of our first meeting, a meeting that took place so long ago that I'd almost forgotten. In the middle forties, towards the end of World War II, I was assigned to do a dance remote from the Crystal Ballroom of the King Edward Hotel in Toronto. The band was Don Turner's and as I arrived to prepare for the show, I met a slightly rotund young man who had a shock of black wavy hair and a wide, toothy smile. He was fiddling around with a record player and I thought he must be a new sound man hired by the hotel. Turned out he was the intermission entertainment. In those early years Liberace played piano concertos to the accompaniment of a symphonic background played on twelve-inch, 78-rpm recordings. Well, we all have to start somewhere and Liberace was biding his time. Who would have guessed that ten years later his chance for superstardom would come with the advent of television. *(early 1966)*

Stompin' Tom Connors

Stompin' Tom Connors was the first Canadian songwriter I know of who purposely uses Canadian place names in his songs, because, as he says: "If the Americans can do it with their country, why can't we?" When it was suggested that Tom might be married on "Luncheon Date," I was at first skeptical; it didn't seem possible that the CBC would approve. I promptly forgot about it and didn't think about it again until early in October 1973 when it was suddenly brought to my attention. I was about to leave for a vacation in Spain and my producer said, "The Connors's wedding is on; it's scheduled for 2 November and you had better be here." Well, getting back was a calamity! Due to weather conditions my flight was grounded in Paris and before I was able to get to London to make my Canadian flight, I had spent an entire night on a French train, taken a rocky boat ride from Dunkirk to Dover, another train to London's Victoria Station, a hectic taxi ride to Heathrow and finally the flight. I made it with twenty minutes to spare. It felt like a speeded-up chase scene in a silent movie. I was in a state of total collapse. Tom's wedding was a splendid affair. It was dignified and done with taste. Tom's sincerity and simplicity gave the event a credibility that no one — not even the critics — could question. Elsewhere in the text of this book I've reproduced the wedding service, but, because of the enormous demand this ceremony brought at the time, here I'd like to repeat Tom's heartfelt words at the end of the service. I had asked Tom what motivated him to have his wedding performed on national television. This was his reply: "Well . . . the way I look at it is this way. Nine years ago in 1964 I was out in this country thinking to myself that my goals that I've had for my life — I'll never see them through. I was a vagabond and at that time I had an awful lot of chips on my shoulder and I cursed an awful lot of people. I really felt down. In nine years it has changed like some kind of a miracle has happened. It was the people I was ready to curse that were the people who, one at a time, came to my side and when they did I couldn't believe it. I thought the least I could do — I couldn't invite everybody in the country, all those who are on my side today, I couldn't invite them to my wedding. I thought doing it on television it would be a great way to give everyone a part of the happiest moment of my life." To me that moment will forever be the most beautiful example of a man speaking through his emotions. If he'd written and rehearsed it, it could never have been delivered with such dramatic impact. It was a statement no actor could have performed with such conviction. *(2 November 1973)*

Lawrence Welk

Someone once labelled me as the "Lawrence Welk of TV talk shows." I was a little uneasy with the comparison until I analyzed it; if it means we're from the same generation, that we appreciate the melodic requisites of music, that we have a sense of showmanship, that we believe there has to be something in life that has gentility, good manners, respect for elders and value for property, then I guess the similarity does exist. Welk and his orchestra were in Toronto for the Canadian National Exhibition and he came up for the program with his widest smile and his great sense of well-being. He was born to a farm family in North Dakota, inherited a lot of rural values and has never forgotten the hard working people of the world. He knows his audience and what it looks for in entertainment. He told me, "If you know your audience and try to please it as much as you can, you cannot go wrong." I asked Lawrence about the criticism he'd taken about his speech – the ungrammatical, unprofessional way in which it was alleged he ran his show. "It used to bother me," he admitted. "But that's me – I know I have a definite European accent, and have difficulty reading a teleprompter. My fans don't tune in to the program to listen to my speech – they want to hear the music. They don't care about all those mannerisms, they realize that's the way I am. It took me a long time to learn that my audience is tolerant of me, but it has become more and more obvious as the years go by." No one can accuse Lawrence Welk of a phony image. He is honest, square-cut, a thorough believer in what his public wants. As someone who understands Welk's personality once said: "Never underestimate the power of a little old lady wearing tennis shoes and carrying a Lawrence Welk record."
(19 August 1974)

Gordon Lightfoot

Our paths have crossed many times in the past, mine and Gordon Lightfoot's. I remember an old TV show called "Country Hoedown" in which Gordon was a member of the chorus – the dancing chorus if you can imagine. Before that, in the fifties, I emceed a variety show from the Canadian National Exhibition's bandshell and Gordon and a partner were playing guitars and singing folk and Western songs. In the years since success and fame have come to Gordon but I have a feeling that success does not sit well with him – he almost seems embarrassed by it. Gordon disparages his talent: "It's a job I have to do and I just settle down and do it." I think Gordon Lightfoot will linger, in decades to come, as one of the world's best-known Canadians. I strongly believe his songs will be a heritage of twentieth-century Canada recognized the world over. I feel privileged to have been present during his lifetime.
(12 March 1975)

Ella Fitzgerald

What can you say about Ella Fitzgerald? It's nearly all been said and it's being said over and over again. I have never seen so much love poured forth by the press, the public and those who have come in contact with Ella Fitzgerald – the person and the performer. I would say at this stage in her life she has reached the epitome of acclaim and adoration. No other graduate of the big-band days has gained this sort of affection with the exception of Peggy Lee who commands it in a different way. Nobody can compare to Ella's position as the world's greatest pop-jazz singer. No wonder she'd called the "first lady of song." Not only has her singing remained on a par with everything she's done in the past, but her human qualities are suddenly being revealed for all to admire. When she comes to Toronto she holds a concert in the Royal York's Imperial Room for the less-privileged children of the city. They are entertained with a specially chosen concert and are served milk and raisins as refreshments. Interviewing Ella Fitzgerald isn't easy; it isn't that you're afraid of her or you're not too sure what mood she'll be in; it's just that she's incredibly shy. She's one of the most retiring people I've ever met. I've seen her lauded by her contemporaries and those who interview her, complimented to the skies. She just tosses her head, glances at the floor and lets the compliments roll off as if it were no special consequence. I remember on one occasion, on the spur of the moment, I asked if she'd sing sixteen bars of a song we'd been discussing. She agreed – and sang with great warmth and dignity. When I realized what I'd done (I made it a point never to ask a performer to entertain if I sensed their refusal in advance) I was flabbergasted that I had ignored my own precaution. Those with her – her assistants and associates – were equally astonished at her ready acceptance. Miss Fitzgerald's eyes are her main concern right now. After serious surgery, she experiences great difficulty in seeing for long periods of time. She often keeps her eyes closed, resting behind thick-lensed glasses. I'm often fascinated by the comparison of a performer's on-stage and off-stage personalities. When some perform, you see essentially an extension of their informal selves. Confidence and assurance they display in dressing room chatter or press conferences is carried with them on stage. In the case of Ella Fitzgerald, you see her on stage completely absorbed and confidently aware that each note she sings is the right one and in its proper place. When she's not performing she is shy, retiring and simply not interested in exploiting herself as a celebrity. *(2 October 1974)*

Johnny Cash

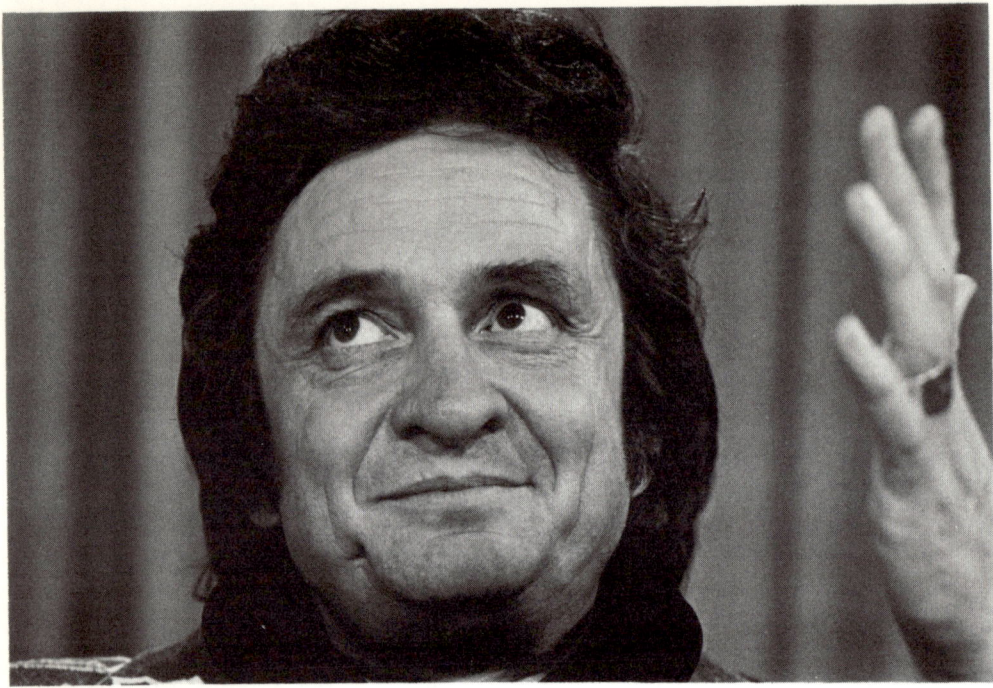

Some people have told me that the program with Johnny Cash was the best "Luncheon Date" interview I ever did. The studio audience was certainly one of the largest we ever had; Johnny had been playing at a local theatre and I swear all members of his local fan clubs turned out to see their idol and get a closer look. I asked Johnny about his well-publicized – and successful – battle with drugs and he told this amusing story. (I think it's a measure of the man's character that he can find humor in the failures of life.) "I had a problem with drugs – amphetamines and barbituates – and I got busted seven times. I didn't realize I'd been in jail so often until I had to fill out a questionnaire at the Hilton Hotel in Las Vegas and down at the bottom it said, 'If you've ever been in jail put down where and what for.' There were five spaces down at the bottom and I had to turn the page over; there wasn't enough room." Johnny is a deeply religious man and says it was his wandering from the faith that got him mired in the drug habit to begin with. But with the help of his wife, June Carter, and "the warm, still presence of God," he gave up the habit entirely. He's obviously very much in love with June Carter: "We've got a great love affair going," he said to me when I asked about his marriage, "so I can't tell you everything." He said he and June never quarrel. "O, sure, we have our differences of opinion," he said, "But we just go away from each other and calm down. We get back together, of course . . . whenever June's ready to see it my way." Cash is a man of great warmth, sincerity and humanity. He radiates a sense of health and vitality that his audience identifies with. And, as he showed on the "Luncheon Date" show, he has a warm, tender humor that causes laughter but no pain. A great entertainer, a great human being.
(27 May 1975)

Cab Calloway

I've been a fan of Cab Calloway since the early thirties. In the early days of talking pictures I saw a film called *The Big Broadcast of 1932* which brought to the screen in his first full-length starring role, Bing Crosby, fresh from the Paul Whiteman orchestra. The movie leaned heavily on stars made famous by radio in those days – Kate Smith, the Mills brothers, the Boswell sisters, Arthur Tracy. "You've heard them all; now see them" seemed to be the rationale. Cab Calloway cavorted, capered and generally acted like a whirling dervish in that movie; he could sing the most depraved songs like "Kicking the Gong Around" and "Minnie the Moocher" and make them sound like childrens' rhymes. When big bands fell from popularity Cab turned to the musical stage and played Sportin' Life in Gershwin's *Porgy and Bess*, a part specifically written for him although he didn't get around to playing it until the fifties. Since then, Cab's been seen in a number of musicals including *Hello, Dolly* with Pearl Bailey and *Pajama Game* with Barbara McNair. I admire Cab's longevity in the world's most precarious business. His work recently in night clubs with his daughters Cecilia and Chris shows the pride he has in a family he had so little time to raise. *(22 January 1975)*

Frank Sinatra Jr.

There are two things about Frank Sinatra Jr. that impress me every time we meet: his "cool" and his conservative attitudes. I've never seen Frank Jr. blow his cool and I'm willing to bet he saves his money. I don't think I ever rattled guests on "Luncheon Date" with tricky or impolite questions; but if I did I know Frank would have fielded them unruffled. Combined with this aplomb is his conservative approach to life in general – to dress, for one thing. In the middle seventies, with men's suits featuring lapels that flared to the shoulder, young Sinatra wore conservatively cut clothing of low-key colors, unflashy ties. His hair is cropped short, almost a brushcut. Even his singing style is conservative; he has not tried to capitalize on the current fad for pop or rock. As a friend once said of Frank Jr.: "He cannot deny paternity so he uses it – but just a little." *(19 March 1975)*

Charles Aznavour

Charles Aznavour is an enigma. He is short of stature; has an appearance that some consider homely. He radiates charisma; and he is an unbelievably magnetic personality. Aznavour is a top international star for all the wrong reasons. He gets down to the roots of a song, brings out the melancholy, the yearning, the frustration and the longing of all of his fans. That's why Charles Aznavour fills halls all over the world whenever he performs. Aznavour has said of himself: "I succeeded because I had to; there are no miracles in my line of work. An artist has what it takes to succeed or he doesn't. Success is the result of a collective hallucination stimulated by the artist. The looks, the voice, the build, the money – none of these really count in the search for success. They can help to start you off but in the end comes the moment of truth and it's the audience reaction that prevails." I admire anyone who can reach the pinnacle of success for all the wrong reasons.
(9 October 1974)

Bob Carroll

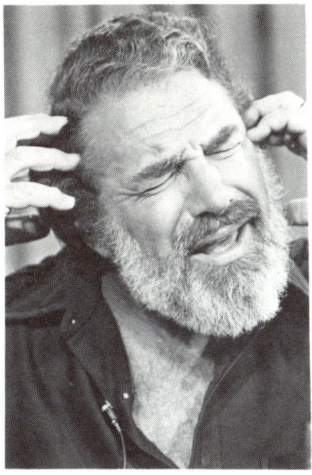

Bob Carroll is a big, bluff guy with a hearty laugh, a firm handshake and a forthright singing style. He always seemed to be starring in *Fiddler on the Roof* each time I interviewed him. Bob got his start as a vocalist with the big bands – Jimmy Dorsey, Charlie Barnet, Glenn Miller's air force band. He is probably the greatest self-promoter of his career that I have ever known. On one occasion, in the dressing room before the show he read an item in the paper that a Hollywood producer was planning to film a biography of W.C. Fields. "I should get that part," he boomed. "I'll call the producer after the show." And, by heaven, he did. I don't think he got the part but he certainly tried. What a showman he is. When you have Bob Carroll as a guest, just turn him loose. He'll never let you down. *(15 April 1975)*

Allan Jones

The mention of Allan Jones's name conjures up memories of those glorious movie musicals of the 1930s. It will come as a shock to some of Jones's fans to realize that at the time of this writing [1975] Allan is sixty-seven years of age. Everyone knows that he's the father of Jack Jones, the pop singer but I assure you they could pass as brothers. Not only has he preserved his appearance; he has retained his zest for life and his superb voice as well. He was my guest on "Luncheon Date" during his appearance in Toronto in the musical, *Man of La Mancha*. Allan made two movies with the wacky Marx brothers – *A Day at the Races, A Night at the Opera* – and two highlights of his career were *The Firefly* from which came the famous "Donkey Serenade," and the 1936 movie of *Showboat*, with Irene Dunne and Paul Robeson. The thing I remember about Allan Jones that was surprising to say the least: *he chews tobacco!* A habit held over from his early days in the Pennsylvania coal mines. He kept a "chaw" stored in his left cheek through the entire interview! *(14 December 1971)*

Leon Bibb

Leon Bibb used to commute to work – from home in Vancouver to work in New York! That's some commute, even once a week as Leon used to do when his show, "Someone New," was running on NBC. While he was involved in this weekly safari Leon used to arrange to stop off in Toronto on the return trip so he could appear on "Luncheon Date." He was one of those guests who could not appear too often. It was always a pleasure to see him. In many ways, Leon reminds me of Harry Belafonte – the songs each sings, the aware social conscience, the probing intelligence – with this small difference: The raw animal magnetism that Belafonte displays is tempered and refined in Leon Bibb's image. His quiet tolerance, the fervor he puts into his work songs, the work he has put into the various humanities (which, incidentally, has brought him numerous awards) make him a welcome resident of our country. On one of his "Luncheon Date" appearances, Leon read the following poem. It reflects, I think, the gentleness and love in his nature and I quote it with his permission.

> Those days of summer
> that speed towards fall
>   we walked the mounded
>   hill
> where the green and gold
> and brown of trees
> cast down shadows in the
> waning evening sun
> Remembering earlier days
> self-same walks and deep
> wanting.
>
> One golden warm late
> August
> with Martha, Les, Jonas,
> Mary and me
> we ran full speed the long
> stretch of road
> that led to Mulligan's back
> meadows.
>
> Sprawled and winded,
> damp with the heat of
> running
> we slowly rose and stood
> at attention
> and applauded that
> glorious sunset.
>
> Those days of summer that
> speed toward fall.

(17 December 1973)

Nelson Eddy

Nelson Eddy was a living legend at the time I met him during his Royal York Hotel appearance in Toronto. How little he had changed from the days of the thirties and forties when he made his spectacular movie musicals. Surprisingly he played down his movie roles. "At the end I shall look back on my life and say, 'Being a recitalist was my most important contribution.' Movies were an accident; I just happened to be in Los Angeles one night and somebody saw my concert and asked me if I wanted to try out for films. I got a job right away as a singer in a picture called 'Dancing Lady.' I made very few movies, only sixteen, but some of them were pretty big hits. Without really meaning to I turned out to be a movie star." And Nelson Eddy still looked like a movie star. He was as tall and straight as a ramrod. His most distinctive feature, his sleek, wavy, blond hair, was now streaked with gray. His face unlined. Nelson Eddy *was* a legend and when he found his career as a concert artist and movie star threatened with the rise of television, he switched careers and became a notably successful night-club artist. *(30 April 1959)*

Tommy Hunter

I'd been trying for years to get Tommy Hunter on "Luncheon Date" but he always refused my invitations by saying that he didn't feel comfortable singing without his own group to back him up. As time went by Tommy obviously acquired more confidence in his own guitar playing and Sonny Caulfield's trio and finally agreed to appear on the "Luncheon Date" show with me. On this day, just three days before Christmas, he sat down beside me and said that he had brought along a couple of people he wanted to audition; and he hoped they'd make a suitable Christmas present for me. He was thinking of using them on his own show, and wondered if he could impose on me to try them out before he did. I knew Tommy was kidding; he was obviously setting me up for some kind of surprise so I played along with him and at last he beckoned to the back of the studio to bring forward a "singer and fiddle player" and from the shadows in the background out came Marg Osborne and Don Messer. As soon as the audience recognized them it roared its approval. Well, from that point the show fell apart – I gave up all pretense of following a schedule. Tommy took over and for thirty minutes he and his "guests" created a happening. Delightful, spontaneous fun. It will be a sad day for Canada if Tommy Hunter is ever lured away from us; he's been a shining light in our entertainment scene for many seasons. I hope he remains so. *(22 December 1972)*

Mart Kenney

"And now, stepping into the spotlight, front and centre, CBC mikeside, here is Mart Kenney and his Western Gentlemen, featuring the lovely and charming Eleanor Bartell asking the musical question . . ." My ears burn and my mind boggles – did we really get away with that? These were the great days back in the early thirties when I used to listen to Mart's music on a program called "Rocky Mountain Melody Time" from Waterton Park in Alberta. Later, "Sweet and Low" was carried Sunday nights on the Canadian Radio Commission's network. Mart Kenney to me was big time. One of my first assignments in Toronto was a dance remote from the roof garden at the Royal York Hotel. To watch this magnificent small band play musical chairs as they doubled on a myriad of instruments was a thrill to see and hear. I still remember some of the original members of the Western Gentlemen: Jack Hemmings, Glen Griffiths, Bert Lister, Jack Fowler, Hec McCallum, Art Hallman and a new girl singer, Georgia Dey. In the years that followed I was the announcer on dozens of Mart Kenney remotes and on his big commercial radio show, "Borden's Canadian Cavalcade." Yes, Mart Kenney was big time. During the years of World War II Mart Kenney was to Canada what Glenn Miller was to the US: great contributors to the morale of the troops and a link of fond relationship between husbands and wives and sweethearts forced to live apart. Mart and his wife, Norma Locke, now live in Mission City, British Columbia, where he is deeply involved in charity work and real estate. *(7 December 1971)*

Tommy Common

Tommy Common was as close to being a regular member of the "Luncheon Date" talent roster as it's possible to be. He's one of the best singers that Canada has produced and he had a standing invitation to come on the show whenever he was in town. He always made a sparkling contribution of personality and charm. In his quest for success in his own country Tommy Common did it the right way. He travelled this country from coast to coast. I guess he has played every city in Canada, adding enormously to his already established popularity. He learned something very early in his career. You don't stay home by the telephone waiting to get work. You get out of town and go where your fans are. Tommy Common is the living proof of the old adage, "Have talent, will travel." *(2 April 1975)*

Buddy De Franco

Without a doubt, Buddy De Franco is one of the most erudite jazz musicians I have ever interviewed. His intellect is immense and his ability to express himself is unsurpassed. He has an unequalled record: For thirteen consecutive years he led both the *Metronome* and *Downbeat* polls as top clarinetist. It's his belief that all youngsters hoping for a career in jazz music should be required to study the classics. "Without it," he told me, "the aspiring musician has nothing but his own musicianship – and that simply isn't enough. Modern music is necessarily an outgrowth of the past. It's the sum total of our heredity and environment." Would that we had Buddy De Franco's equal in every music school in the country. *(30 November 1972)*

Maurice Solway

Ordinarily, Maurice Solway is a neatly dressed gentleman, his suits well tailored and his tie correctly with perfection. The costume he wears in this picture is part of his makeup for his role in the short movie, *The Violin*. I guess almost everyone had heard of *The Violin's* success – a perfectly charming little story about an impoverished fiddler who teaches two small boys the appreciation of music from an old and battered violin. This film revolutionized Maurice Solway's life. From a stolid and somewhat routine existence as a symphony violinist and a studio musician, Maurice became a dedicated, almost frenetic promoter of the movie. He travelled with the film to schools and libraries; he cornered friends and acquaintances and burbled out the story of the film's latest success. Just after this "Luncheon Date" appearance Maurice took off for Hollywood to watch the Academy Awards presentation in which *The Violin* had been nominated in the short subject division. Unfortunately, the film lost out but that doesn't make it any less of a triumph. I've known Maurice since 1938 and he was a neighbor for twenty years. Success in a new career – it doesn't come to many of us that late in life. *(21 January 1975)*

Vic Damone

Vic Damone seems to me to be an original hard-luck guy. Leo Durocher once said, "Nice guys finish last." Vic is just that – a gentle, nice person. He makes the Durocher epigram fit close, but not completely. He is anything but last in his profession. The trouble with Damone's niceness is the quality of naïvete that goes with it – he himself admits he's never been a good businessman. He's always trusted people, he's had himself tangled up in deals in which he often comes out the loser. His bankruptcy case alone – *who* could cope with a $750,000 debt in back taxes alone? As if his financial problems aren't enough to worry about, Vic had to contend with two sad, unhappy marriages and the accompanying gossip – and think of the additional strain of having two ex-wives take their own lives. Damone has taken a lot of heartbreaking innuendo about that and it's unfair. The women died long after divorcing Damone and after they'd resumed separate lives of their own. I don't know how the man has stood up against it all through the years – singing beautiful songs, raising young children and competing successfully in the most risky of all professions. I think Vic Damone, in spite of the jinxes he's encountered, has an incredible will power. He is the consummate showman who allows nothing to affect his performance. There's a line in the song "MacArthur's Park" that seems to describe Vic Damone's struggle with fate: "I shall win the worship in their eyes and I shall lose it." His faith in his new-found religion BaHai has given him great courage and strength. Perhaps that and the loyalty of his fans give him the confidence so necessary to carry on in the face of adversity. He's one of the greatest in his field, which two of his contemporaries, Tony Bennett and Frank Sinatra, constantly acknowledge. *(11 May 1973)*

171

Guy Lombardo

There was a time when the name of Guy Lombardo was a laughing matter in music-industry magazines such as *Metronome* and *Downbeat*. Today, nobody says anything disparaging about Lombardo's music; he has outlived the critics and stuck fast to his beliefs about what comprises the best in popular dance music. An occasion I'll always remember was when Guy appeared on "Luncheon Date" with his original drummer from London, Ontario, George Gowans. George started out with Guy and his brothers in the early twenties and had retired a few years ago to the quieter life but when Guy's nephew, Lebert's son, left for younger fields, George leaped at the opportunity to return to his old chair. He said he's never been happier and will never retire again. Elsewhere you will have passed another photograph of Guy Lombardo as he appeared on stage at the Maple Leaf Gardens for the old "Fitch Bandwagon" show in 1943. He has matured gracefully in the more than thirty years, but Guy Lombardo is still playing the music he knows his fans expect him to play. It's curious how I find the old success stories fascinating. *(19 September 1974)*

Stan Kenton

Stan Kenton is a unique man of modern music. He has had a band since the early forties and nurtured his special brand of big-band jazz all through the decades. Throughout his career Kenton has been harassed by critics and public alike: Kenton's music has been a puzzler to many. What is he trying to do? He's often been compared to abstract painting. I can remember hearing Kenton's band from the Balboa Beach Ballroom in California in the early forties. He had a sharp, jerky, syncopated rhythm then that I called a "pogo stick beat" which was his first identifiable sound. Then he got into broader chord structures with wall-to-wall dissonances that would jar the eardrum. But, no matter what his style, Kenton has poured every ounce of his creativity into his music and shows no sign of easing up. "I don't want any other kind of life," he told me. "On the road I am my own master – I don't have a phone, an office and I don't own anything. I am a free agent. My life style makes me a complete human being." Stan Kenton used to be accused of a certain verbosity; I can remember concerts at which he regaled the audience with long, detailed descriptions of his music. He's over that now; he gets along these days on much less wordage and many more "Innovations." Throughout the years Stan has had the courage to be different and because of that he never stops growing. *(12 July 1974)*

Harry Belafonte

I've talked with Harry Belafonte on two or three occasions, the most recent being May 19 1974 during a week when he appeared at Toronto's O'Keefe Centre. He was a quiet pensive man on this visit. He didn't talk much about his career although his career probably concerned him more than he would let on. He was constantly worried about finding good material. He deplored the lack of what he called "a renaissance period" in current music. He even went beyond music and asked where are all the new painters, the new poets, and

most of all the new Lightfoots, where are all the contemporary composers writing about the conditions of the world as they are? He was deeply concerned with the flacidity of the social condition. Then he thought of his friends. I remember he talked about the people he knows like Brando, Poitier, Norman Jewison – they're all in different parts of the world now whereas they used to get together frequently, talk on 'phones, visit back and forth. I don't know where Harry Belafonte is at this date of writing. I have not read of concert tours or other activities. I remember at the time he was here he wanted to get out of the business for a year or two. Maybe that's what he's done. He wanted to think. He wanted to contemplate "his present and his future" he said. What disturbed him the most while he was here was a review in one of the Toronto newspapers which I remember he answered in the letters-to-the-editor page in brilliant rhetoric: "I welcome the creative criticism of responsible critics. What I do not welcome and truly abhor is the irresponsible, inaccurate journalist who diminishes the dignity of the term critic by totally obviating the facts for the sheer exercise of taking a cavalier swipe at an artist, an artist who has taken years to develop a style, a uniqueness of presentation."

Another quote that displays the perspective of Harry Belafonte was one I took from an aircheck of an interview he did with me in the middle 60's when he spoke about the Vietnam war and the mad race the conflict was accelerating. It was spontaneous, beautifully worded and from the heart of a worried man: "My son is quite concerned about how long it will go on. When he's eighteen will he be swept up by a military-minded nation, be taken off to some foreign land, be part of some unnecessary mischief? All of these things play on my day-to-day thoughts – my sense of responsibility to my country – my debt to the world community. How can I as a public figure alleviate some of these frustrations and give some sense of direction?"

Harry Belafonte may be a tower of strength when he appears on stage, but when he sits down and talks he is a very vulnerable person when he wrestles with the agonies of the world. *(19 May 1974)*

6

★★★★★★★★★★★★★★★★★★★★★★★★★★★★★

I RECALL REACHING...

... a certain conclusion as far back as 1970. In the spring of that year I said to myself on my birthday, "I'm fifty-five years old." (Not an advanced age by any means but a mellow time of life when one's youthful exuberances are tempered by experience.) "Do I want to be doing this sort of thing in my sixties?" In other words, I asked myself how long could I continue "Luncheon Date," how long could I go on in the full glare of the public eye doing a chancy, nerve-wracking talk show that seemed destined to go on and on and on. Surely in those precarious years from sixty to sixty five thought should be given to taking the foot from the accelerator and slowing the tempo before the full stop of retirement. In a real sense, I suppose, the decision to abdicate from "Luncheon Date" was made in 1970 – though I certainly did not articulate it that baldly.

It's true – the hearing impairment had become a strain and there was a constant battle to conquer my concern for the program. But there were other considerations as well.

Since its beginning, I had been uneasy about the kind of guests who were attracted to the show. As I've mentioned, in the early days we operated as a no-budget, one-camera show; so close to the poverty line did we come that I often wondered, whimsically, if we couldn't qualify for a LIP or OFY grant. No longer was it possible to cruise the Four Seasons' dining room to corral guests; every minute of TV time had to be programmed and planned in advance. In a word, we needed guests, at least twenty to twenty five a week.

When the word got around, we were inundated with suggestions. Every public relations representative in Toronto was on the phone offering his client for "Luncheon Date" exposure. We were hurting for guests so we listened. As a result the program became a forum for freeloaders. In terms of numbers, the travel profession led the way. Every agency that entertained a visiting fireman – here to extoll the merits of his resort area as the holiday haven of the world – was welcomed on the program. They were followed by magazine writers who were promoting an article in this or that month's issue of a periodical. Then came the book publishers and the movie publicists. There were the service clubs – there wasn't a sponsor of a pink tea, a bazaar or a tag day that didn't want air time to talk about his project. Then there were the little theatre groups; these were the hardest to turn down because we sympathized with their courageous attempts to advance local theatre with no budget for advertising.

Don't get me wrong; I am *not* saying we didn't get good interviews from these occasionally attractive people. The problem was that with no budget to pay guests, we had to rely on the PR types to provide free guests who might – or might not – turn out to be interesting on their own. It was impossible to tell beforehand whether we were simply providing a free plug for a book or a movie or whether we were supplying entertainment for a national audience.

As we gained experience the show improved. We were able to cut down on the travel people, the bazaar ladies and the little theatre. We acquired a second camera and a small budget for paying certain guests who qualified as professionals. But it would have taken a vastly increased budget to attract celebrities to Toronto for a "Luncheon Date" appearance alone; we still had to rely on the publicists to get us "names" such as Henry Fonda and Melvyn Douglas. We managed to camouflage the blatant plug for a movie or stage show by extensive research on the personalities and, as I became more experienced in my role as interviewer, I was able to conduct the conversation in a way that skirted the obvious pitch. Every day, in the early evening, my hard-working researchers delivered huge envelopes containing dossiers on the next day's guests. I did more homework for "Luncheon Date" than I ever did while I was in school.

The feeling of being "had" and exploited haunted me in

In "Luncheon Date's" latter years it often seemed to me that I spent at least five hours on the phone for every hour on camera.

177

those early "Luncheon Date" years. It was only after long experience that I acquired more confidence in my own conducting of the show that I was able to live with it comfortably.

A new problem popped up in 1974; three other television stations in the Toronto area scheduled talk shows in and around the same noon-hour spot that "Luncheon Date" occupied. Now Toronto is not the whole of Canada but it is the largest single English-speaking market in the country; and with four programs of similar format occupying the same time of day, the arithmetic of the situation demanded that the "Luncheon Date" concept would be up against new and strong competition. The pain of that realization was heightened by the fact that our competitors were simple studio shows with no studio audience, no musical group, none of the "show-bizzy" technical set-up "Luncheon Date" demanded. It was a formula we were locked into and no immediate changes could be contemplated.

Aside from the sudden glut of noon-hour talk shows on the market, another unsettling thing occurred. A magazine article appeared commenting on the relative merits of daytime television in Canada. "Luncheon Date" was rated as one of the lowest of the low. There had been murmurings on occasion in letters-to-the-editor columns about the show being intentionally male chauvinistic – these gave me little concern. But here was a story, with an obvious feminist slant, that held in high praise all the banner-waving women's lib shows while at the same time shooting "Luncheon Date" down in flames. It jerked me up to the realization the way things were going. Instinctively, I knew "Luncheon Date" and I were beaten and it was a matter of time. Male dominance in TV-host roles was fast diminishing.

Also, I began to have some doubts about the audience appeal of "Luncheon Date." For years our regular mail had indicated that the great body of our devoted fans were older citizens, the fifty-five-plus group. For one thing, most of them were home at noon and watching TV had become part of the midday ritual. Many of our viewers were confined in rest homes and convalescent hospitals; for them "Luncheon Date" came around as regularly as their luncheon trays. I was pleased and proud of the loyalty the fans showed.

More recently, I began to worry about myself: If this was the audience attracted to "Luncheon Date," did it mean that I, too, was getting old? Was I playing it too conservatively, was I discarding *good* new ideas along with the *bad* new ideas? I have always felt that broadcasting has a responsibility to bring programs to all levels and age groups of society. I wondered about the responsibility of appealing to the younger audience so they wouldn't be left with the impression that the show was for nostalgists only.

These considerations, added to my hearing impairment increased my uneasiness.

As I've already mentioned, I discussed my misgivings with

Sonny Caulfield – a tower of strength on which I did considerable leaning.

*Luncheon Date at Warwick Castle, England.
I was born 400 years too late!*

a CBC official in December of 1974. I asked to be relieved of the program after its current season expired. But I did not resign. I stated that I was ready to take on any new duties the corporation thought I could handle. I made it very clear that I was prepared to work on camera or off, on mike or off. I was even prepared to become a "desk jockey," if something functional and interesting came along.

Having spoken my piece, I left on a month's vacation. I returned at the end of January 1975 to find that news of my intension to leave "Luncheon Date" had become rumor material. Blake Kirby, a television critic for Toronto's *Globe and Mail,* was clinging to the story like a leech: He repeatedly pestered the CBC to reveal its plans for Glover. I think there was a reason for this: On Christmas Day 1974 Kirby devoted a whole column to discussing all the Toronto-area talk shows. Glover's show was so bad, Kirby said, that it placed "far back in the pack, and often in last place." (A real honey of a gift to find under one's Christmas tree.) Several paragraphs later he about-faced and quoted audience ratings to show that "Luncheon Date" was a close second in Toronto-area homes. I twitted Kirby on the air for his blatant, biased and humorless attack; I've been told that he watched the show, seething. I have a sneaking suspicion he was rubbing his hands with glee at the rumors of my departure. When I returned from my vacation I was inundated with phone calls from Kirby seeking verification of the rumors. Bewildered by all the fuss and having just returned to Canada and not having spoken to anyone yet, I said I would leave any comment to the CBC.

The CBC finally admitted that the program would end at my request in June 1975 and that a new program, as yet untitled, would be developed to fill the time slot. It would be, the CBC hinted, a variety show with a greater degree of "audience participation" than "Luncheon Date" displayed. I was left with the uncomfortable feeling that the corporation had already decided to change the program and that my withdrawal from it conveniently provided them with the perfect out.

I'd be less than honest if I said I was less than affected about the apparent disinterest displayed by the CBC in relocating me within the organization. Certainly I wanted something less arduous than what I had been doing but as the months rolled by, I saw no alternative to the most menial of staff duties which I was preparing myself to accept.

In almost any other business a valued employee would be offered an alternative or some incentive to stay. It has been my experience – and this comment is strictly personal – that there is little communication within the ranks of the CBC. You'll never be fired but you'll be allowed to drift until frustration and futility eventually destroy you unless you came to terms with it. Luckily I did not have to anticipate this. A proposal in April from radio station CKEY offered me a chance to do what I wanted – radio as I used to know it. I chose retirement from the CBC rather than chance the consequences of dwindling morale and gradual decay.

All of which sounds bitter. Not so, not so. I have great respect and admiration for much of what the CBC is and has done. In a personal sense I am deeply grateful to the CBC executives back in 1938 who were prepared to take a flyer on a twenty-three-year-old, largely untried announcer from Western Canada. I'm equally grateful to the program people who listened to my eagerly described ideas for new programs and actually allowed me to put them on the air. And for everyone of my co-workers who helped give reality to my ideas I cannot find praise enough. My one mistake may have been that all of my programs – radio and television – were based on the personality approach. I'm sure that the programs often gave the impression that Glover was a one-man egomaniac independent of all others. Only those people who have worked with me can know how far from the truth is that impression: Each of them will know this "thank you" is meant for him and her personally.

I've had a tremendous sense of personal gratification from my work, a deep inner satisfaction that my broadcasting has been as good as I can make it. I've always accepted the failures, as well as the successes, as my responsibility alone. That's all you can ask of thirty-seven years of anything.

But, have I any regrets? Not many. Looking back on a TV series that ran longer than most I know of, I try to analyze what held it together. Why did it continue to be renewed year after year? I have a couple of theories on that. For one thing, it was unusual. It was unlike anything else on Canadian day-time television. It was a talk show, similar in structure to the American product, but loose and freewheeling with enough Canadian character to make Canadian viewers feel it was part of their lives. Throughout the many changes since its beginning: the three-person production staff and one black-and-white camera, to the greatest change: a light-entertainment endeavor in full color with music, song and some comedy: throughout eleven and one-half years of daily, live, spontaneous, unrehearsed content – not once did I allow the Canadian image to falter. Certainly we were peppered with American names and in some cases, guests who may have appeared to be of local interest only. But, the stigma of hogtown Toronto, so rampant throughout the

The Glover family in 1972. Our daughter Sharon (Mrs. Scott McNeill) is at the top and Barbara between Violet and me.

rest of the country, was never allowed to intrude. Bob Blackburn of the Toronto *Sun* said it best in his column: "All the best interviews came his way when the subjects were passing through town, but he has always been conscious of the rest of the country (hell, in some respects, he *is* the rest of the country) and merely tried to share the excitement of Toronto with viewers elsewhere, rather than lording it over them..."

Regrets? Only that I'll miss the excitement generated in the earlier years. We did the impossible – three people producing an hour, and sometimes an hour and one-half of programming five days a week. That drew gasps of disbelief from seasoned producers who had "staffs of thousands" for a weekly, prime-time show. But we had freedom to operate up there in the middle of the day. And we were alone. The air was yet to be flooded by the myriad of low-budget, single-guest talk shows which began to surround the lunch hour during the last year of "Luncheon Date's" life.

Certainly, the show was efficiently staffed in its latter years, but the same excitement was no longer there. Sure, the chaos of the early days with guests not showing up or cancelling out entirely at the last minute was a stimulant. We were tiny then and making something out of nothing was a miraculous accomplishment.

When "Luncheon Date" became bigger, with a more big-time aura and a moderate budget to help us along, it was unreal that we still had to endure the same "hope-to-God-everybody-will-show-up" atmosphere that prevailed every day. But, being a live show meant "the show must go on" in every sense of the word – it continued to be a harrowing experience.

All this is one reason why the day of the "live" entertainment show is almost extinct. Even the spontaneous Americans have found this out. The "Tonight Show," the last of the American nightly talk-variety shows, is taped a day in advance with all the editing and bleeping taken care of.

At "Luncheon Date" it was gangbusters every day. Every show trod the fine line between success and disaster. I don't suppose a viewer realizes the hazard of working like this, but I simply felt, "enough is enough." I want to breathe a little before I approach that "final glide path in the sky."

Another thing: (although this is personal opinion and I can't prove my theory) I strongly suspect "Luncheon Date" would never have lasted (or at least my association with it) had I been a freelance performer. I am a product of the older school of CBC staff broadcasting: the self-sufficient, the creatively-in-command, completely individualistic type of broadcaster of the old MacDougal, Whitteker, Maitland, Holly, Ferguson period. I was among the last of my kind. The days of thinking up a program idea, presenting it for approval, getting same, choosing the theme, selecting the

This was the scene as "Luncheon Date" signed off the air for the last time, 27 June 1975, after a nineteen-year run on radio and TV.

music, writing the script or relying on your ad lib ability, getting the show on the air and maintaining its standard – those days are over.

    We now have experts to pick the records, experts to wave the cues, experts to dream up the ideas and experts who have made studies of public taste, experts who know exactly what every viewer and listener to CBC are waiting to see and hear. We old timers are thinning out, we're not needed anymore.

"Personality" programming is a thing of the past. True, there are night-time blocks of programming devoted to specialized categories, but for the most part, it is now the public affairs approach. The CBC is news-and service-oriented. The current local radio and TV management make it quite evident that formalized entertainment programming of the escapism type headlined by a personality is no longer prevalent. The world around us in its chaos and confusion is now the prominent radio fare. Everything must be probing, in-depth and "investigative" (I love that word).

However, being staff means you're never heartlessly replaced. In my case I was safe with "Luncheon Date." Management knew the program would never cause embarrassment or controversy. They also knew that as long as I was happy with the program I was performing a worthwhile function. But, I also knew instinctively that the old haphazard format on which "Luncheon Date" was based ("live" by the grace of God) was rapidly becoming obsolete. The control must now come from the department and the control booth. The performer no longer is the key manipulator of the show.

So, although I originated the idea and carried it through, I knew inside that when I left, so would the concept.

I think I can safely predict that no announcer (for that was still my group classification in the eyes of the CBC) will ever be allowed such freedom again.

This is the age of the contract performer. He is signed, he performs his function and he is out. Simple, clean, no loose ends. With a staff person, management is obligated. There is a person with seniority and pension benefits to consider and to place.

"Luncheon Date" especially, brought me much – the fruits of intelligence and wit from some of the world's most brilliant minds. The meeting face to face with people celebrated in all walks of life. It gave me the opportunity to prove to myself that I could "hang in there" under all circumstances, a chance to bring amusement and information to people and, above all else, give comfort and company to the lonely who count the television set their only close friend. As one woman wrote me just before the program concluded, " 'Luncheon Date' brings so much of what is going on out there into the homes of so many. Authors, actors, all the interesting people – even if one cannot read all the books, see all the plays, go to all the entertainment spots, one sees the creators of it all, the very precious, vital human beings."

To all the gentle people who comprised my audience, I say again what I said on the last program, 27 June 1975: "It's been a distinct pleasure."